Contents

Foreword

This White Paper is the culmination of a lengthy and broadly based consultation process.

For the past three years there has been intense debate on the most appropriate framework for the future development of education in Ireland. The extent and depth of the dialogue is arguably unprecedented in our history. The debate has also been characterised by a number of unique and innovative features, specifically the National Education Convention in October 1993 and the subsequent Roundtable discussions on intermediate education structures and school governance, in 1994. These initiatives involved, for the first time, structured multi-lateral dialogue among all the major partners in education on crucial issues affecting the development of education. They contributed substantively to enhanced mutual understanding and, I hope, have facilitated a more robust consensus in support of key changes.

The White Paper builds on this consultative process. It reflects a widespread desire among all the partners in education to take stock of the achievements and trends in educational provision and practice and to chart future directions. It builds upon the best of these trends and sets out a framework for the development of education into the next century, against the background of a rapidly changing and evolving society.

The White Paper describes a comprehensive agenda for change and development. It seeks to give an empowering sense of direction to all of the partners in education. It outlines policy directions and targets for future development including significant organisational developments. Within an enabling framework, it seeks to allow for flexibility to meet particular needs and circumstances, respects legitimate rights and responsibilities among the partners and the different levels of the educational system, and clarifies the role of the Minister and the Department of Education in educational policy and provision. It also indicates the manner in which an appropriate legislative framework will be provided for key aspects of educational provision in the future. This White Paper heralds a major programme of legislation.

The approach to the implementation of change will be important. Effective change does not occur instantly. The implementation of the policies and decisions described in this White Paper will require sustained effort over time from all involved in education. The White Paper provides the strategic direction. However, carefully planned implementation strategies will also be necessary, consolidating the best achievements of the past, while adapting to changing needs and circumstances in the future. It is essential that there is a firm commitment from all the partners to the achievement of change, to respond to the changing needs of students. Changes will continue to be implemented on a partnership basis, involving consultation with all the concerned interests where this is necessary and appropriate.

The Government will aim to provide, during its period of office, the resources for the development needs identified in this White Paper, within the framework of the budgetary parameters set out in the *Government of Renewal* policy document, including the acceptance of the Maastricht Treaty convergence conditions. The amount which can be made available in any given year will have to be decided by the Government in the context of its financial position and its other public expenditure priorities at that time. In this context, the Government will have the opportunity to consider any potential which may exist to reallocate resources within the education sector in the light of demographic changes.

The implementation of the strategy set out in this White Paper is not contingent on the availability of resources alone. It will also require leadership and commitment across the education system and many important developments in the White Paper will improve the education system without additional cost. The strategic directions set out in this White Paper reflect the need to ensure the greatest possible benefit from the available resources.

The ultimate objective of the strategies set out in this White Paper is an education system which will provide every student with fulfilling educational experiences at every stage in a lifetime of learning. As our society becomes more complex, the capacity to learn continuously will determine each individual's life chances and decisively influence the quality and prosperity of our society.

Niamh Bhreathnach, T.D.

Niamh Bhreathnach, T.D.,
Minister for Education.

12 April, 1995

Part

1

Philosophical Framework

Philosophical Rationale for Educational Policy and Practice

1

Introduction

Education makes a fundamentally important contribution to the quality and well-being of our society. This White Paper addresses itself to the policy framework that can best embrace the diverse and multiple requirements for educational action in the future. The need for and importance of such a framework are widely accepted. In setting out a framework, it is important to provide a philosophical rationale which, far from being merely a theoretical or ceremonial exercise, systematically informs policy formulation and educational practice.

Although it is scarcely possible to secure total agreement on all the essentials of such a framework, it is important to gain as much shared commitment as possible before resources are committed to major new initiatives, and indeed to continue the search for further consensus in a spirit of genuine dialogue between the partners. In this regard, the National Education Convention played an important role. It also highlighted the need for continuing attention to a coherent philosophical rationale. The **Report on the National Education Convention** stated: "*Within an improved overall policy approach and framework, attention to a philosophy and aims for the education system should be a matter of priority*" (p. 7). The **Report** concluded: "*Given that every educational action unavoidably presupposes a philosophy of some kind or another, the provision of an adequate philosophical rationale, from which both structures and practice draw their coherence and strength, remains a priority*" (p. 7).

The expression of explicit and coherent principles which win widespread commitment is a fundamental task in realising the major initiatives described by this Paper and securing the resources needed to support future development.

Principles of Approach

The development of a philosophical rationale for the role of the State in education is informed by the following principles:

● the State's concern is with a number of key considerations which should underpin the formulation and evaluation of educational policy and practice – principally, the promotion of quality, equality, pluralism, partnership and accountability

- the State is obliged to protect and promote fundamental human and civil rights, in accordance with the Constitution, national law and relevant International Conventions, including the United Nations Convention on the Rights of the Child

- the articulation, nationally, of a statement of broad educational aims, which focus on nurturing the holistic development of the individual and promoting the social and economic welfare of society, including the provision and renewal of the skills and competencies necessary for the development of our economy and society

- within a national framework, individual schools, colleges and partners in education are entitled and empowered to nurture and promote their particular values, traditions and character, and to set out their philosophical approaches.

Developing a philosophical rationale, which informs State activity in relation to educational policy making and provision, is important for a number of reasons:

- it contributes to a more cohesive partnership and strong consensus in policy making and implementation by setting out the key elements that inform policy and practice

- it promotes transparency and greater accountability, provides a rationale for the allocation and use of resources and makes it easier to evaluate educational provision

- it establishes a solid foundation for the clarification of the respective rights and responsibilities of the partners

- such clarification, in turn, instils greater confidence and vibrancy into the relationships among the different levels of the education system – national, regional and local, as well as the individual institution, college or school – on the basis of well-defined roles and functions.

A rationale for the articulation by the State of guiding principles in education is clearly identified in the ***Report on the National Education Convention*** *"The state has a responsibility to set out educational principles and rights within which educational institutions may set out their philosophical approach, while respecting such rights"* (p. 7).

Education and the State

The State's role in education arises as part of its overall concern to achieve economic prosperity, social well-being and a good quality of life within a democratically structured society. This concern affirms fundamental human values and confers on the State a responsibility to protect the rights of individuals and to safeguard the common good. Education is a right for each individual and a means to enhancing well-being and quality of life for the whole of society.

The State must therefore seek to create, promote and support the conditions within which education can realise its potential in society. The democratic character of this society requires education to embrace the diverse traditions, beliefs and values of its people. Irish education is profoundly influenced by the long commitment of the Catholic and Protestant churches and other religions in the provision of education. The Vocational Education Committees have made a significant contribution to the development of education. In addition, Ireland has benefitted from a distinguished tradition of higher education. All have, from their varying traditions, served Irish students and society well.

The State has a duty to respect the legitimate interests of the various partners in education and support the distinctive character of individual schools and colleges. They, in turn, have a corresponding obligation to respect and support the principles and rights upon which a democratic society is based.

The development of the education and skills of people is as important a source of wealth as the accumulation of more traditional forms of capital. National and international bodies have identified the central role of education and training as one of the critical sources of economic and social well-being in modern society. This is the logical outcome of the increasing centrality of knowledge and skills in shaping economic organisation and national competitiveness. Interlinked with these trends is the emerging economic necessity for life-long learning, given the speed with which knowledge and skills become outdated. For these reasons, expenditure on education and training is an investment in economic growth and improved social cohesion.

Links between education and the economy, at national and institutional level, are important. This has been recognised by successive Governments, the social partners and various expert bodies. The contribution of education and training to economic prosperity has been underlined in successive national understandings with the social partners and in independent studies carried out by, for instance, the National Economic and Social Council and the Organisation for Economic Co-Operation and Development. These developments have placed education at centre stage as part of more broadly based economic and social policies. The Government is committed to continuing this process. The Government's concern with this key dimension of education complements and reinforces the fundamental contribution of education to individual and social development. Enhancing the contribution of education and training to economic prosperity requires an independent and dynamic educational system which is systematically linked to the economic planning process.

Economic activity is increasingly dependent on the knowledge and skills of people and their capacity to learn continually throughout their lives. Thus, investment in education is a crucial concern of the State to enhance Ireland's capacity to compete effectively in a rapidly changing international environment.

Educational Principles

Educational principles and rights are derived from the fundamental aim of education to serve individual, social and economic well-being and to enhance quality of life.

Pluralism

The human capacity to develop is universal, lifelong and multi-dimensional. While the capacity to develop is part of human nature, each individual has unique learning needs. Individuals differ in the way they learn. Their learning is influenced by physical, mental, economic and social factors. Hence, the State should serve the educational rights of its citizens to participate in and benefit from education in accordance with each individual's needs and abilities and the nation's resources, within a framework which entitles individual schools and colleges to promote their philosophical values.

Policy formulation in education should value and promote all dimensions of human development and seek to prepare people for full participation in cultural, social and economic life. Old divisions of 'liberal versus vocational education' should be transcended in order to elicit the full range of each student's potential.

Living a full life requires both knowledge and skills appropriate to age, environment, and social and economic roles, as well as the ability to function in a world of increasing complexity and to adapt to continuously changing circumstances without sacrificing personal integrity. This requires the development of a sense of individual responsibility to oneself and to the different dimensions of community – to the family, to local and work communities, to the State, and to the European Union. It entails the full, holistic and lifelong development of the person. The policy-making framework should embrace the intellectual and cultural heritage of the past – the knowledge, beliefs, values and traditions transformed and transmitted through succeeding generations.

Equality

The principle of equality is at the heart of the protection of individual rights and the promotion of community well-being. Where participation and achievement in the education system are impeded by physical, mental, economic or social factors, the State should seek to eliminate or compensate for the sources and consequences of educational disadvantage. As the *Report on the National Education Convention* stated, *"the key concern [is] to enable each and every pupil to make the most of [their] potentials; to overcome limitations wherever this is possible; to mitigate their effects wherever it is not"* (p. 8).

The education system for the future should have a philosophy that embraces all students, female and male, on a basis of equality. A sustaining philosophy should seek to promote equality of access, participation and benefit for all in accordance with their needs and abilities. Measures to promote equality will include allocating resources to those in greatest need, providing appropriate support systems, and changing the tangible and intangible qualities of the system itself to cater for the diverse educational needs and interests of the population. It will also include strategies for the earliest feasible intervention to support children at risk of educational failure and will develop specific measures to continue special supports for such children throughout their education.

Partnership

The learner is at the centre of the educational process. The other principal participants are collectively referred to as the partners in education – parents, patrons/ trustees/ owners/ governors, management bodies, teachers, the local community and the State: Other participants, including the social partners, businesses and the professions, should also be recognised as having legitimate interests in the system. Effective partnership involves active co-operation among those directly involved in the provision of education and the anchoring of educational institutions and structures in the wider communities they serve. This also enhances the contribution of education to the democratic process by enabling communities to actively influence the decisions which affect them.

The development of a strong commitment to partnership will require improved co-operation among schools, coupled with better regional co-ordination and planning of educational provision. This co-operation will recognise the autonomy of individual schools, but equally will recognise the benefits of constructive co-operation in enhancing the welfare of all students and making the most effective use of available resources.

To this end, the State should seek to promote and support an effective balance among the contributions of all those involved in education while recognising the integrity of the educational process itself. This balance is best achieved through an approach which recognises different traditions and approaches, which respects legitimate rights and responsibilities, but which also encourages a fruitful learning from each other and the discovery of new possibilities. Effective partnership also requires increased transparency and accountability, in order to allow the partners to exercise their rights and to be accountable for their responsibilities.

Quality

Students are entitled to the highest possible standard of teaching and to be facilitated in the attainment of the highest quality of learning. The State should ensure and promote the highest standard of education and learning for all. This entails a variety of interdependent factors, including the quality of the curriculum, teaching and assessment and the quality of teachers in schools, school and institutional management, and planning processes. In addition to the determination of a policy framework for each of these areas, the State should also develop rigorous procedures for the evaluation of educational effectiveness and outcomes, with due regard to the legitimate autonomy of individual institutions.

Quality is brought about by maximizing the efforts of all those responsible for the education of students and by co-ordinating all the structures of the system so that centres of education, from pre-school to university, are effective – that is, places where effective teaching, learning and research take place and where the highest standards of achievement are obtained by every student, appropriate to their ability.

Accountability

Education is a major beneficiary of Government spending. In 1995, Government expenditure on education will amount to over £2 billion. The activities of educators, of schools and colleges, and of the Department of Education touch daily the lives of close to one million students.

Because education occupies so central a position in individual and social development, appropriate processes must be operated at various levels, to evaluate the effectiveness of educational policy, provision and outcomes. Such processes will include arrangements for:

- accountability to those served by education, including parents, students and the wider community

- accountability to the national and regional authorities.

There are many legitimate competing demands for resources in education; the amount of money available for education is limited. To ensure the best possible use of available resources and to allow for full public accountability, the State should ensure that effective systems are in place at national, regional and local levels for evaluating the effectiveness and efficiency with which resources are used. Procedures should also include the clear identification of accountability at national, regional and local levels. Value for money is essential if students and the community are to get the best possible benefit from the available resources.

Parents

The Constitution acknowledges that the primary and natural educator of the child is the family. Article 42.1 states that it is the inalienable right and duty of parents *"to provide, according to their means, for the religious and moral, intellectual, physical and social education of their children."* Although most parents choose to avail of formal schooling for their children, the role of the family in the child's development remains central up to and into adulthood. Parents bring to the children's education the unique expertise derived from intimate knowledge of the child's development, of her/his child's particular needs and interests and of circumstances outside the school.

The parental role confers on them the right to active participation in their child's education. This entails parents' rights as individuals to be consulted and informed on all aspects of the child's education and their right as a group to be active participants in the education system at school, regional and national levels.

Parents also have responsibilities. Parents should nurture a learning environment, co-operate with and support the school and other educational partners, and fulfil their special role in the development of the child.

School Ethos

Every school has a tangible quality defined by its physical and organisational structures. However, it also has the critical, intangible character called 'ethos', which encompasses collective attitudes, beliefs, values, traditions, aspirations and goals. It is important to emphasise that the ethos of a school is an organic element, arising, first and foremost, from the actual practices which are carried on in that school on a daily, weekly and yearly basis.

School ethos is of legitimate concern to parents, given their rights and responsibilities in the education of the child. These educational rights and responsibilities reinforce the school's interest in fostering and protecting its particular ethos. The protection and promotion of the school's ethos is also a particular and legitimate right of those patrons, trustees, owners and governors to whom parents entrust the education of their children. While each school may properly nurture and support its particular ethos, it is also obliged to acknowledge and reflect the principles and requirements of a democratic society, respecting the diverse beliefs and ways of life of others.

The rights of parents in their children's moral and spiritual upbringing are particularly significant for a school's ethos, and for the values and beliefs of teachers. Where the values and beliefs of teachers conflict with parents' rights to choose their children's moral and spiritual upbringing, the education system should decide in favour of the rights of parents, with due regard to the principles of justice appropriate to a democratic society, including the principle of applying the minimum necessary restrictions on teachers.

Societal and Individual Development through Education

Proceeding from the foregoing considerations, this White Paper sets out the following statement of educational aims, incorporating individual and societal development, as a basis for active reflection by the partners, as a guide to policy formulation, and as guidelines for inclusion in the daily practices of teaching and learning in schools and colleges. The aims are:

- to foster an understanding and critical appreciation of the values – moral, spiritual, religious, social and cultural – which have been distinctive in shaping Irish society and which have been traditionally accorded respect in society

- to nurture a sense of personal identity, self-esteem and awareness of one's particular abilities, aptitudes and limitations, combined with a respect for the rights and beliefs of others

- to promote quality and equality for all, including those who are disadvantaged, through economic, social, physical and mental factors, in the development of their full educational potential

- to develop intellectual skills combined with a spirit of inquiry and the capacity to analyse issues critically and constructively

- to develop expressive, creative and artistic abilities to the individual's full capacity

- to foster a spirit of self-reliance, innovation, initiative and imagination

- to promote physical and emotional health and well-being

- to provide students with the necessary education and training to support the country's economic development and to enable them to make their particular contribution to society in an effective way

- to create tolerant, caring and politically aware members of society

- to ensure that Ireland's young people acquire a keen awareness of their national and European heritage and identity, coupled with a global awareness and a respect and care for the environment.

Ireland has a rich cultural heritage. The education system has an important role to play in its conservation and development. Education can do this by inculcating a strong sense of pride in being Irish and by emphasising the Irish language and traditions, Irish literature, music and other cultural activities.

Education empowers individuals to participate fully and creatively in their communities. Time spent in education is not just a preparation for life, but is also a lengthy and important period of life itself. For this reason, the importance of collective, as well as individual, development is a key educational aim. Increasingly in the future, continuous education and retraining will be a feature of people's lives, with initial education forming a foundation which will be built upon regularly. The education system should help to build up and empower communities economically, socially and culturally.

The achievement of these aims should inform the internal school community, in all its aspects, and also the links between the school or college and the wider community.

Conclusion

The following sections of the White Paper elaborate approaches to different policy issues in education informed by the principles described in this section. The objective is to achieve an active engagement among the partners in the process and the challenges of change which we are facing, deriving from a consensus on the broad purposes and aims of education.

Part
2

Provision of Education

2 *Primary Education*

Introduction

Each child is entitled to an education and learning environment, which facilitates the nurturing of her/his full educational potential, in all its richness and diversity. All schools should aim to create such an environment for their students, to the greatest extent possible. The school environment should be a caring one, in which each child's right to a joyful and safe childhood is guaranteed at all times. The achievement of these aims will inform national, regional and school planning processes.

Pre-Schooling

Preamble

Although children in Ireland are not obliged to attend school until the age of six, 65 per cent of four-year-olds and almost all five-year-olds, are enrolled in the infant classes in primary schools. Ireland shares a maximum entry age of six years with the majority of States in the European Union, where entry ages range, in practice, from four to seven years. Because primary schools in Ireland admit children from the age of four, *"much of what is considered pre-schooling in other countries is already incorporated in the primary school system in Ireland,"* as the Primary Education Review Body noted (p. 72).

There is a limited number of compensatory programmes available for three-year-olds, including programmes for children of travellers and children in an inner-city Dublin area. In addition, there are a number of pre-school programmes for children with special educational needs.

The health authorities also give grants to voluntary bodies, to provide pre-schooling for children with disabilities and for disadvantaged groups. These are mainly in nurseries and in community play groups, run by voluntary agencies.

The Child Care Act, 1991, acknowledges the links between health and education measures. It provides for consultation with the Minister for Education in regard to regulations concerning the health, safety, welfare and development of pre-school children availing of pre-school services.

Rationale

The Government's strategy for education is characterised by the hallmark of equality. When social or economic disadvantages impede a child's potential, justice and equality imply the need for specially designed measures that seek to alleviate or eliminate the sources and consequences of this educational disadvantage.

Pre-school intervention is based on three principal considerations:

- early childhood experiences are important for the child's development

- entry to formal schooling is a major transition for children, particularly those from disadvantaged backgrounds

- early disadvantages affect the child's enduring experience within formal schooling, because such disadvantages tend to be both persistent and cumulative.

Targeted educational intervention during the pre-school years can ease the transition to formal school. Well-designed interventions at this level also influence positively the child's short- and long-term educational performance. Supporting research stresses the importance of parental involvement in maximising this effect. The **Report on the National Education Convention** noted that *"research strongly supports the effectiveness of such interventions, provided the teachers/leaders are well-trained and the curriculum is both suitable for the age groups and enriched"* (p. 108). Reflecting the strong feeling of participants, the **Report** added: *"such pre-school interventions should be closely linked to both the family/community and the school"* (p. 108).

Pre-school programmes should provide both care and education, they should have appropriate adult/child ratios, and they need continuing monitoring and evaluation. Children participating in specific pre-school intervention programmes will continue to be supported as necessary throughout their schooling by the range of specially targeted intervention measures at first and second levels, for example, the home-school links programme, additional staffing, support services and enhanced capitation rates for schools in disadvantaged areas.

The Early Start Programme

The **Government of Renewal** policy document commits the Government to the further expansion of pre-school education. A pilot pre-school intervention programme, Early Start, has already been established in designated disadvantaged areas and this initiative is supported by the European Union. The **Report on the National Education Convention** recorded *"a substantial welcome for government proposals on targeting pre-primary educational interventions on schools in disadvantaged areas"* (p. 108).

The Early Start philosophy views learning as a guided discovery through a series of structured activities, aimed at the harmonious development of the whole child. Students are respected as active agents in their own development within a learning environment which encourages creative self-expression through language, music, drama, art and physical education. The pre-school curriculum makes language and numeracy skills a priority and includes an appropriate introduction to the Irish language.

Early Start involves parents at three levels: parents belong to an advisory group in each centre, parents participate in the everyday running and organisation of the centre and parents join their children in many of the centre's activities. This creates a shared exchange of expertise between the centre and the parents, helping parents to develop a fuller understanding of their child's learning needs and allowing the centre's activities to benefit from the parents' unique experiences and insight.

Building connections between the pre-school and other developments in the local community strengthens the impact of pre-school intervention. This places Early Start within the wider context of the Government's Local and Urban Renewal Development Programme, particularly with reference to disadvantaged communities. Early Start is one element of an integrated approach to education, training and employment initiatives for the entire community.

Future Development

The overall aim for the Department of Education's pre-school programmes is to compensate for background deprivation. These programmes support the optimum development of the child and her/his smooth and confident transition to full participation in the formal education system.

An expert monitoring committee has been established to oversee the implementation of the Early Start pilot project. The purpose of the committee is to evaluate the effectiveness with which pre-school objectives are being achieved and the effectiveness of approaches adopted. The committee will advise the Minister on the most effective way forward, including alternative models, to achieve the overall aim.

In addition, the pre-school pilot project will be independently evaluated on a systematic and thorough basis by the Educational Research Centre, Drumcondra, with particular emphasis on the effectiveness of the curricular methodology, aims and objectives.

Future development of pre-school provision will take account of these evaluations. A critical dimension in future pre-school provision will be to ensure systematic follow-through of support for children so that the benefits of pre-schooling are not lost, but rather, are maintained and built upon for as long as necessary throughout each child's education.

The Primary Education System

Primary education is founded on the belief that high-quality education enables children to realise their potential as individuals and to live their lives to the fullest capacity as is appropriate to their particular stage of development. A good primary education gives children a firm basis for future participation in and progression through the education system.

The primary education sector comprises primary schools, special schools and non-aided private primary schools. It serves almost 500,000 children. There are just over 3,200 primary schools and 115 Special Schools. The primary schools, which account for the education of 98 per cent of children in the primary sector, are staffed by over 20,000 teachers. More than 50 per cent of the schools have four or fewer teachers. In addition, there are seventy-nine private primary schools which receive no State funding.

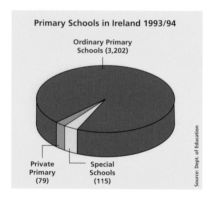

Primary Schools in Ireland 1993/94

Ordinary Primary Schools (3,202)

Private Primary (79)

Special Schools (115)

Source: Dept. of Education

The current and capital costs of primary schools, including the full cost of teachers' salaries, are predominantly funded by the State and supplemented by local contributions. In addition, special funding arrangements are in place for some schools, for example, in disadvantaged areas and for children with special needs.

Curriculum

Operating Principles

The term "curriculum" encompasses the content, structure and processes of teaching and learning, which the school provides in accordance with its educational objectives and values. It includes specific and implicit elements. The specific elements are those concepts, skills, areas of knowledge and attitudes which children learn at school as part of their personal and social development. The implicit elements are those factors that make up the ethos and general environment of the school. The curriculum in schools is concerned, not only with the subjects taught, but also with how and why they are taught and with the outcomes of this activity for the learner.

The way in which the curriculum is defined, planned, implemented and evaluated crucially influences the quality of education provided. The proper management of the curriculum should be such as to ensure the quality of provision in schools, that is, to provide students with a range of understanding, knowledge, skills and attitudes best suited to their personal development, and to enable them to make a productive contribution to the society in which they live.

There are different levels of responsibility for the development and implementation of the curriculum. At national level, the curriculum is formulated by the Minister for Education, on the advice of the National Council for Curriculum and Assessment and the Department of Education oversees its implementation through its inspectorate. At school level, the particular character of the school makes a vital contribution. Adaptation of the curriculum to suit the individual school is achieved through the preparation and continuous updating of a school plan.

Effective curriculum planning and implementation require clear aims and values. They also require well-defined learning objectives and integration of the different activities which contribute to their achievement. Curriculum planning should be a continuing process involving planning, observing, assessment and revision in the light of experience.

Principles

The primary school curriculum is based on the following principles:

- the full and harmonious development of the child, with due allowances made for individual differences

- the central importance of activity and guided-discovery learning and teaching methods

- teaching and learning through an integrated curriculum and through activities related to the child's environment.

These principles identify a child-centred approach, outlined in the 1971 review of the primary school curriculum, which radically changed the philosophy and methodology of primary education from its previous emphasis on subject-centred, didactic teaching. Primary education now emphasises the central position of the individual child and promotes a curriculum related to the child's needs and interests.

Review of the Primary Curriculum

The child-centred principles of the 1971 curriculum were endorsed in 1990 in reports by the Review Body on the Primary Curriculum and the Primary Education Review Body. The following year, the Minister for Education invited the National Council for Curriculum and Assessment to conduct a continuing review of the primary curriculum, while retaining the basic principles adopted in 1971.

The review is taking account of the rapid social, scientific and technological change which is taking place, and of Ireland's position in the European Union and in the wider world. It is also aiming at a more precise statement of objectives, where possible, in terms of student behaviour and attainments. In addition, the National Council for Curriculum and Assessment will make recommendations on the time allocations necessary to achieve the stated objectives for each subject taught. This will be particularly important, because of the need to balance a wide range of curricular objectives with the amount of school time available.

The National Council for Curriculum and Assessment will continue to advise the Minister on all aspects of the curriculum, to provide curricular objectives and guidelines, and to advise on assessment methods and on transition arrangements from primary to second-level schools.

Particular Aims of the Revised Primary Curriculum

Special emphasis will be given to a number of areas within the revised curriculum.

Literacy and Numeracy

A fundamental aim of the revised primary curriculum will be to enable students to communicate clearly and confidently in their first language through speech, reading and writing and to acquire basic numeracy and problem-solving skills. The ***Report on the National Education Convention*** endorsed the view that *"a central task of the primary school is to provide pupils with levels of literacy and numeracy that will be adequate for further education and for their development as individuals who are able to function effectively in society"* (p. 69).

A significant minority of students do not acquire satisfactory levels of literacy or numeracy while at primary school. This means that these students cannot access or benefit from the primary curriculum, are most likely to drop out of school and are most likely to become long-term unemployed. The revised curriculum will place particular emphasis on overcoming this problem. **The objective will be to ensure that, having regard to the assessment of their intrinsic abilities, there are no students with serious literacy and numeracy problems in early primary education within the next five years.**

The achievement of this ambitious, but vital, objective will be addressed in the revised primary curriculum. This will be done through the following means: a greater emphasis on the early identification of children with learning difficulties; adapting the curriculum to individual needs; the use of appropriate assessment methods; expansion of the school psychological service; home-school links programme; in-career training programmes for teachers; and analysis by schools of their literacy and numeracy programmes and staff development policies.

In future, all schools will be required to include in their school plans a strategy, with defined objectives and associated performance measures, for achieving basic literacy and numeracy targets. The provision of enhanced resources and programmes and other support services to schools will be based on a clear strategy of intervention agreed between schools and the education boards, in accordance with national guidelines. This will ensure the more effective use of resources and will facilitate the evaluation of the effectiveness of intervention measures.

The Arts

The Government affirms the centrality of the arts within educational policy and provision, particularly during compulsory schooling. This commitment promotes an education system which encourages young people to be positive, responsible and active agents in society by emphasising their personal and social creativity. Artistic and aesthetic education are key elements within the school experience of young people; such a nurturing of creativity assists the young person to become a tolerant, critically aware and socially committed citizen who can live with confidence in the world.

A good arts education develops the imagination, as a central source of human creativity, and fosters important kinds of thinking and problem solving, as well as offering opportunities to symbolise, to play and to celebrate. The development of critical judgement encourages a sense of personal responsibility in the young person. Such education is distinguished by a number of benefits:

- the opportunities provided for the encouragement of innovation and the development of intuition

- the balancing and linking of reason and feeling in artistic experiences

- the use of material and technology in a highly disciplined way

- the particular immediacy of an arts experience, enabling the student to encounter at first-hand experiences that may otherwise be remote

- the wide range of personal and social development encouraged by the variety offered by different arts experiences, ranging from highly personal experiences to those which are collective in nature

- the development of self-reliance and responsibility for decision-making in the young person.

A broadly based arts curriculum, which will include music, dance, drama, painting, poetry and story-telling, will be drawn up in the context of the review by the National Council for Curriculum and Assessment. This creative and performing arts curriculum will identify appropriate learning objectives in the arts for various developmental levels from infants to sixth class.

Science

Scientific and technological developments have an enormous influence on our society, whether through their economic and social effects or though their impact on individual lifestyle. In a fast-changing world, it is important that people are able to understand such innovations and to evaluate their implications. Apart from their wider effects, science and technology play an important role in the student's intellectual formation, complementing educational experiences in the arts and humanities. International comparative surveys have shown that the overall science achievement of thirteen-year-old students in Ireland is low compared to a number of other OECD countries (see *Education at a Glance, OECD Indicators* 1993, p. 167, Table R3 (A)).

The development of a new science programme will form an integral part of the review of the social and environmental programme now in preparation. This new programme will foster the development of scientific thought processes and approaches to problem solving, with an emphasis on critical and constructive thinking which will have applications in other parts of the curriculum. Schools will be encouraged to place greater emphasis on the scientific aspects of the social and environmental programme, particularly in the senior classes.

European Awareness Programmes

A further aim of the revised primary curriculum will be to develop an appreciation of European life and culture. **In the context of a European awareness programme, students will be introduced to European languages, life and culture.** This programme will introduce students to various European languages, other than English and Irish, and instill in them an understanding and appreciation of European life, art and culture. It will foster links between Irish schools and those in other countries of the European Union, through, for example, the Socrates programme (see Chapter 17).

The Irish Language

In the Constitution, the Irish language as the national language is the first official language. The promotion and preservation of the language has been an important aim of every Irish Government since the foundation of the State. The language occupies a central place in the culture and heritage of the Irish people. Learning Irish also helps to develop linguistic skills and so encourages students' facility in acquiring other languages. Attitudes to the Irish language at home and in society are determining factors in assessing the benefit which students will draw from the opportunities to learn Irish offered by their schools.

It is the function of the educational system to provide the means for students to learn the Irish language and to make them aware of its inherent value. Students' proficiency in the language is crucially related to their motivation and the opportunities for them to use the language outside the classroom. These, in turn, depend on the attitudes of parents and the community, the extent to which the home encourages the learning and use of Irish, and how far Irish is used or its use encouraged and appreciated in the community. Without significant support from both home and community, even the best language programmes and pedagogical methods will have limited success.

Too frequently there has been an undue focus on the amount of time spent on the learning of Irish rather than on standards reached. For the future, the focus will be on the specification of attainable learning objectives for each primary school level rather than on time spent. The minimum objective in the revised curriculum will be that, **on completion of their primary education, students will be able to conduct a simple conversation in Irish and will have acquired a knowledge of the basic structures of the Irish language, as a foundation for further study at second level, and an awareness of Irish history and culture**. As part of its general review, the National Council for Curriculum and Assessment, with the assistance of Institiúid Teangeolaíochta Éireann, has been given the task of examining the present programmes for the teaching of Irish in primary schools and of proposing more clearly defined learning objectives for different age-levels.

The Promotion of Health and Well-Being

The revised primary curriculum will also aim to develop students' physical ability and their knowledge of, and responsibility for, their bodies and their health, within the framework of the health-promoting school. The health-promoting school will adopt a positive approach to enhancing the social and personal development of students, including interpersonal skills. **It will implement a broadly based programme of physical and health education which will promote the well-being of its students and incorporate a new emphasis on diet, hygiene, safety, and relationships and sexuality education.** (See also Chapter 13 which deals with the promotion of health and well-being in schools.)

Religious Education

The revised curriculum will reiterate the right of schools, in accordance with their religious ethos, to provide denominational religious education and instruction to their students, while underpinning the constitutional rights of parents to withdraw their children from religious education instruction. In the context of the revised curriculum, the ***Rules for National Schools*** and the ***Teacher's Handbook*** will be reviewed to **ensure that the Constitutional rights of children are fully safeguarded**. Therefore, while recognising and supporting the denominational ethos of schools, all schools will be required, in their management and planning processes, to ensure that the rights of those who do not subscribe to the school's ethos are protected in a caring manner.

A sensitive balance is required between the rights, obligations and choices of the majority of parents and students, who subscribe to the ethos of a school, and those in a minority, who may not subscribe to that ethos, but who do not have the option, for practical reasons, to select a school which reflects their particular choices. In very many instances, the concerns of the parents and students are dealt with successfully, but problems have arisen in some cases. In this regard, the **Report on the National Education Convention** noted that: "*The dilemmas and challenges posed for policy-makers and school authorities require not only dialogue at school level but the development of "good practice" guidelines by a suitably qualified and representative working party convened by the Department*" (p. 33). **Such a working party will be convened in the near future.**

Implementation of the Revised Primary Curriculum

The detail of the revised primary curriculum will be introduced through a process of dissemination and briefings at school, regional, and national levels.

The commitment of teachers, parents, patrons, management bodies and all involved in education is essential, if the objectives of the revised curriculum are to be achieved. The maintenance of a high-quality education depends particularly on the professional development and adaptation of teachers. A comprehensive in-career development programme will be offered to teacher, parent and management bodies. Pre-service education for teachers will also be modified.

Students with Special Needs

Context

The **Report of the Special Education Review Committee** defined students with special educational needs as including "*all those whose disabilities and/or circumstances prevent or hinder them from benefiting adequately from the education which is normally provided for pupils of the same age, or for whom the education which can generally be provided in the ordinary classroom is not sufficiently challenging*" (p. 18).

All students, regardless of their personal circumstances, have a right of access to and participation in the education system, according to their potential and ability. The achievement of full equality of access, participation and benefit for all students will entail positive intervention at all levels in favour of those minorities who experience particular difficulties.

The objective will be to ensure a continuum of provision for special educational needs, ranging from occasional help within the ordinary school to full-time education in a special school or unit, with students being enabled to move as necessary and practicable from one type of provision to another. Educational provision will be flexible, to allow for students with different needs, at various stages in their progress through the educational system.

The Special Education Review Committee has made detailed recommendations on meeting the needs of students in each category of disability. A special task force has been set up within the Department to implement the report's findings, as resources permit.

Assessment of Needs

Each school will be responsible for presenting in its school plan its policy on student assessment. This policy will provide for the identification of students with special needs and will describe the school's proposals for helping them, with the co-operation of parents.

Although the special educational needs of some students are identified before they start school, classroom teachers carry the main responsibility for identifying and responding to learning difficulties. The assessment procedure will focus on the identification of the student's potential rather than on her/his perceived limitations. The school Psychological Service will be expanded to support teachers in this task and to ensure that every child with learning or behavioural difficulties has access to help, at the earliest possible stage. Co-ordination of the school Psychological Service in each area will be the responsibility of the education board. Each education board will co-operate closely with the relevant health board in relation to the School Health Service and clinic-based assessment services in its area.

Action

The details of each student with a special disability will be entered in a national data base, to facilitate the planning of provision for all students with disabilities. **Each education board will have a statutory responsibility for all students in its region who have been entered on the national data base,** and will co-ordinate educational provision, including support services, for these students.

A number of ordinary primary schools will be designated by education boards as centres where students with particular disabilities may be educated. Existing special schools will fulfil an expanded role as schools dealing with a variety of disabilities and as regional resource centres. Each student with a disability will be assigned to the nearest appropriate special school in the region, whether or not s/he attends the school. If it is decided that s/he will attend an ordinary school, the student and her/his parents will still have access to the support services available in the special school.

Multidisciplinary consultations, to which parents and students will have a right of access, will review the educational provision for each student at least every three years. The decision-making process, in relation to the placement of a student in an ordinary and/or a special school, will be a collaborative one, made by the parents and professionals involved, with the objective of providing what is best suited to the child's development and needs.

In the case of the small minority of students with significant learning difficulties, where special provision is required, **the education board will make arrangements for the writing of a statement of special educational needs for these students on an individual basis.** The statement will identify the nature of these needs, the special educational provision required to meet them, and the school in which they can be most effectively met.

The National Council for Curriculum and Assessment will advise on the setting up of curriculum development projects for students with special educational needs. To accommodate educational provisions for children with disabilities in mainstream schools, the development of the curriculum will allow for flexibility, addition and adaptation. The curricular needs of all students in specialist classes, units and schools will be reviewed continually, based on age, ability, needs and aspirations. Appropriate in-career development for the teachers of students with special needs will be organised.

Children of the Travelling Community

Approach to Policy

Travellers are a community whose culture has deep historical roots within Irish society. Each distinctive group within a democracy has a right to participate fully in its educational system and to have its traditions respected. Traveller children will be encouraged to enjoy a full and integrated education within the schools system. All educational institutions which receive public funding have a responsibility to provide for travellers who wish to attend them.

The placement of traveller children in special schools and classes will be done only on the basis of special educational need. If they need extra help, this will be given, as it is to other children with learning difficulties, through withdrawal from the ordinary class for a limited period, or through support teaching within the ordinary class.

The participation rates of traveller children at all levels of the education system *"are unacceptably low for a democratic society"*, as the ***Report on the National Education Convention*** concluded (p. 127). The policy objective is that **all traveller children of primary school age be enrolled and participate fully in primary education, according to their individual abilities and potential, within five years.** Responsibility for achieving this objective will rest with the education boards, supported by specific actions as follows:

- the inclusion in school plans of admissions policies for travellers, in accordance with national and regional guidelines

- the continuing development by the National Council for Curriculum and Assessment of appropriate curriculum and assessment procedures to meet the special needs of traveller children, including the provision of appropriate texts and materials

- the continuing development of the visiting teacher service

- the provision of modules on traveller culture in teachers' pre-service and in-career development programmes

- comprehensive and regularly updated quantitative and qualitative surveys of traveller education

- the monitoring of school attendance patterns.

Teaching Methods

Principles

The principles of the primary curriculum emphasise child-centred learning through project work, guided discovery activities and group-teaching. These principles form the basis of teaching methodology. Within the curricular framework, schools and teachers are responsible for choosing those methods best suited to particular subjects and individual school circumstances, balancing teacher-directed intervention and guidance with the recognised need for student activity and discovery methods.

Teachers will continue to exercise professional freedom in their choice of effective teaching methods. The National Council for Curriculum and Assessment will advise on a wide range of teaching methods to suit the varying needs of students across the curriculum.

Quality of Teaching

Teachers' professional competence is a key element in successfully implementing the schools' curriculum. That competence is informed by:

- knowledge of and commitment to the principles, aims and objectives of the curriculum

- the ability to adapt to change in the curriculum

- skill in selecting and using recommended teaching approaches and methods and in evaluating their effectiveness

- the capacity to function effectively as a member of a school staff.

To achieve the revised curricular objectives, necessary changes to teaching methods and approaches will be incorporated in teachers' pre-service training and in-career development programmes. A particular focus will be to develop approaches and methods needed to tackle disadvantage and to reach the targets specified in this chapter.

Assessment

Aims

Assessment is of central importance in monitoring and enhancing the quality of education at school and national levels. It helps teachers to collect reliable information on the strengths and weaknesses of students and to accurately and systematically assess progress at various points in the individual student's school life. It is not an end in itself and should not dominate the work of the school. The purpose of assessment is not to rank schools. Most teachers currently assess their students' progress, mainly in the cognitive areas. Assessment practice ranges from observation, classroom discussions and homework to the use of standardised tests, both norm- and criterion-referenced. Standardised assessment is currently being used to evaluate reading and mathematics in many schools on an annual basis from first to sixth class.

The ***Report on the National Education Convention*** recorded that "*there is a general concern among practitioners and the Department of Education that achievement standards in schools should be raised and, in particular, that serious problems of under-performance should be tackled. It is clear that, under present conditions, some children slip through the net and are not being identified until it is too late. The fact that there is no external examination that might bring such failures to light through the primary school and right up to the age of fifteen years, serves to underline the need to establish procedures for obtaining information on the functioning of primary schools. The need for a system of quality assurance will be all the greater in the future, if greater authority is devolved to individual schools*" (p. 71).

Approach to Assessment

The ***Report*** also recorded that "*there is general agreement that all schools should have, as part of their school plan, a system for the evaluation of the progress of individual pupils. The system should specify procedures for assessment and for reporting assessment results for individual pupils to parents. The assessment results should also be considered on a whole-school basis. There is an obvious place for standardised tests in such a system to provide normative and diagnostic information as a basis for devising teaching programmes*" (p. 72).

All primary schools will be required to develop a policy on assessment within the framework of the school plan. This policy should ensure uniformity and continuity- of approach between classes and within the school. Under the direction of the school principal, students will be assessed by their teachers at the end of first and fifth class in order to evaluate the quality of their learning and to identify any special learning needs that may arise. Many teachers will also continue to assess students at the end of each school year.

Satisfactory attainment levels in literacy and numeracy are essential for students, in order to participate fully in, and benefit from, all other learning activity in the primary school and to ensure that they are not impeded in their subsequent progression through the education system. In recognition of this, a specific target has been set to address literacy and numeracy difficulties among primary school children. To allow for the systematic evaluation of the achievement of this objective, the Educational Research Centre, in co-operation with the National Council for Curriculum and Assessment, will be asked to advise on and develop appropriate standardised forms of assessment for these core competencies to be applied at all levels in the primary school. The outcomes of such assessments will be available to the education boards and to the Department of Education in appropriate form, to allow for the monitoring of the achievement of standards in literacy and numeracy.

Nature of Assessment

Assessment should be diagnostic, formative and continuous, and geared towards providing information for teachers, schools, students and parents which will help to improve the quality of education and educational outcomes. This means that assessment should be viewed as an integral part of the curriculum and of the teaching and learning process in every class. Assessment should combine informal teacher assessment with the judicious use of standardised tests, without making disproportionate claims on class time or activities.

Based on the curriculum, assessment should cover comprehensively all parts of the curriculum and all the various elements of learning – the cognitive, creative, affective, physical and social development of students, their growth in self-esteem, the personal qualities being acquired, and the acquisition of knowledge, concepts, skills, attitudes and values. With this approach, assessment should identify the student's learning strengths and weaknesses as a basis for decisions about her/his further learning needs. Effective assessment will help to overcome difficulties and lead to improvements in performance.

Assessment Outcomes

Assessment data for each student will be recorded on standard student profile cards, designed in accordance with guidelines issued by the Department of Education, following consultation with relevant interests, including the representative organisations for parents, teachers, school managers and patrons.

Parents will be guaranteed statutory right of access to their own children's school records and will be informed of their children's assessment outcomes. They will be able to give and to receive useful information about their child's learning, needs and social context through discussions between parents and teachers.

Aggregated assessment outcomes for each school, in accordance with nationally agreed guidelines, will be available on a confidential basis to boards of management, to education boards and to the Department of Education for the purpose of quality assurance, the identification of special learning needs and the targeting of resources. These data can be of assistance in enhancing the quality of education regionally and nationally.

In addition, at national level a system of monitoring standards, based on the regular assessment of the performance of a representative sample of schools, will be established to provide information on an aggregate basis to the Department of Education and to the general public. Schools participating in this survey will not be identified publicly.

Teachers will be provided with pre-service education and in-career professional development in assessment methods, as well as in the recording and effective communication of assessment results.

Time in school

Research findings indicate that the amount of time that students spend in organised learning activities critically influences their academic performance and all-round development. The total amount of time spent in school depends upon the length of the school day, the length of the school year and the number of years in which the student attends school.

Primary School Year

In 1990, the Primary Education Review Body carried out a detailed study of the length of the primary school year. The Review Body was concerned to ensure that students' entitlement to the minimum number of official school days was guaranteed. However, the Review Body noted that most schools operated for less than the required minimum number of teaching days because of such practices as early and special closures. In response, the Review Body recommended that the attention of boards of management be drawn to the necessity of complying with all rules pertaining to the duration of the school year.

The integrity of the school year and the school day will be preserved. **A circular about current rules will be issued to all primary schools**, on the basis illustrated by the following model:

Days		
School in operation for teaching		183
Standard number of closings:		
(a) Saturdays and Sundays	104	
(b) Permitted Vacation Days	56	
(c) Public and Religious Holidays	16	
	176	176
Remaining days		6
		365

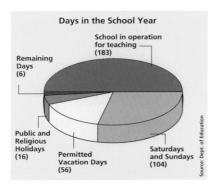

An Approach to Policy

In future, **there will be a statutory obligation on all boards of management to ensure that the prescribed minimum number of teaching days per annum and the minimum number of hours per day are observed**. From time to time, the Minister will prescribe the minimum number of teaching days and hours.

In the context of the present minimum, the six "remaining days" will be used for school-related activities, such as curriculum development, school planning and staff development, as well as for special closures.

Each board of management should assess each proposal for the closure of its school, in order to determine whether it is in the best interests of the students. Each board should bear in mind that the reasons that might warrant the closure of a school for student-teaching purposes need not necessarily justify the non-attendance of teaching staff to engage in other essential or desirable school activities. Each board, therefore, should ensure that the opportunities offered by such closures are fully availed of by the teaching staff working together to further the aims of the school. Each board should also give parents at the beginning of each year a calendar of events in the school, including closures.

Providing for Schooling

Diversity of Schooling Provision

In recent decades, Irish society has been undergoing significant change affecting all areas of society. Most parents avail of denominational education for their children through the medium of the English language, but others seek alternative schooling provision. Examples of this are the emergence of parental movements which favour all-Irish or multi-denominational education for their children. A Muslim school has recently been established in Dublin and it seems likely that parents and parent groups will seek an increasing diversity of school types in the future. While this development is in line with the growing plurality of Irish society, it poses an additional challenge to the financing of the system by the State, particularly when student numbers are declining. It will not be possible in all circumstances, particularly outside the larger centres of population, to provide the choice of schools reflecting different ethical or cultural traditions to match the choices and preferences of all parents.

At present, in the case of national schools generally, the patron or promoter must provide a site for a new school. The Department does not provide any grant aid towards this. Consequently, the Department has limited legal rights to a disused school. Among these is a right in some circumstances to a refund in respect of the capital grants towards the cost of the buildings. By contrast, the Department provides the full cost of sites for all-Irish national schools. Demographic changes and the growth in demand for all-Irish schools and multi-denominational schools have increased the need for interchangeability in the use of school buildings. Multi-denominational national schools and all-Irish primary schools are given initial recognition on a temporary basis for a number of years subsequent to their establishment. As a result of this, the promoters must provide temporary accommodation without the aid of capital grants during the period of temporary recognition. This is often a hardship on the promoters of such schools and may militate against their establishment. This requirement was originally imposed to ensure that State investment was made available for viable school projects. However, because – for historical and practical reasons – new denominational school projects have been grant-aided from their inception, the requirement is seen as discriminatory against new school projects other than those promoted by the main religious denominations. The ***Report on the National Education Convention*** recorded *"unanimous agreement among participants at the Convention that the rights of parents to multi-denominational education should be respected and facilitated"* (p. 31).

Ownership of New School Buildings

In future, full recognition and full entitlement to capital grants will be given to all schools, including all-Irish and multi-denominational schools, from the date of their establishment, as soon as the Minister is satisfied in each case that there will be a continuing need for the school.

The conditions for this recognition will be that the patron or patron body makes an application to the education board, that the education board is satisfied that the new school is necessary for the needs of the area, and that the Minister has formally sanctioned the recognition. This will allow permanent accommodation to be provided at an earlier stage and early recognition of new multi-denominational and all-Irish schools is listed as a priority in the *Government of Renewal* policy document.

In relation to identifying and securing accommodation for all-Irish and multi-denominational schools, the Department of Education has initiated discussions with the religious authorities so that vacant school buildings can be made available, on reasonable conditions, to groups of parents where there is significant evidence of sufficient continuing demand for such new types of schools. In this regard, the *Report on the National Education Convention* stated that "*it would appear unacceptable for the state to have to buy back school buildings at current values, where the historical costs were, predominantly, originally paid for by the state*" (p. 32).

In future, education boards will own new school buildings and property for leasing to different groups of patrons and trustees, in order to provide for the educational needs of each region. This is in line with the practice in other member States of the European Union of providing publicly owned buildings for compulsory education. The *Report* noted that "*Ireland was seen as unique in requiring citizens to provide privately owned accommodation for this purpose*" (p. 31). These leasing arrangements will be made in accordance with national guidelines and will be subject to the approval of the Minister. All buildings for new schools will be provided in this way.

Rationalisation

Context

The issue of school size and the provision of appropriate school facilities for students are complex and sensitive matters. Policy making has to take account of a variety of important factors, including demographic trends, curricular policies and local community needs, as well as social and cultural factors. The *Report on the National Education Convention* concluded "*that good planning for school provision, in the context of significant demographic decline and new curricular policies, is one of the major issues of this decade [the 1990s] and needs sustained and skilled attention by all authorities involved*" (p. 34).

It is projected that the number of students enrolled in primary schools will have declined from a current level of just over 490,000 to under 430,000 by the year 2001. This rapid demographic decline poses a major challenge for the provision of primary schooling.

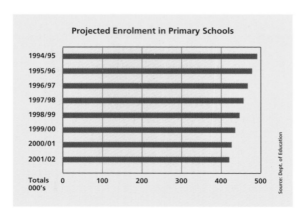

The past thirty years have witnessed a consistent decline in the number of smaller schools and a marked increase in the number of larger schools. Whereas in 1965/66, 90 per cent of schools had three teachers or fewer, these schools now constitute only 42 per cent of the total number of schools. Much of this change reflects altered economic patterns at regional level and the effect of a rationalisation programme for primary schools during the 1960s and the 1970s.

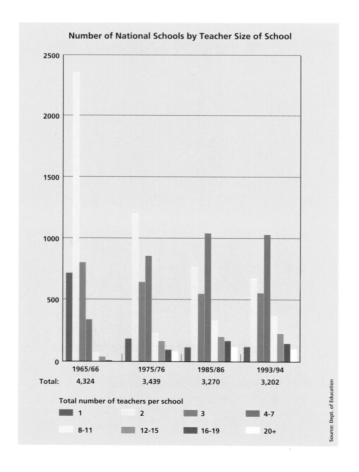

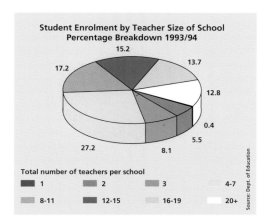

If the projected demographic decline were to be evenly distributed, however, it is estimated that by the year 2000 the number of schools with three teachers or less would have increased significantly, while the number of one-teacher schools would have more than doubled.

Approach to Policy

The advantages of small schools were considered at the National Education Convention. They include less frequent lengthy journeys for young children, the intimate character of small schools, and the social interaction among parents and teachers promoted in a small community.

Among the disadvantages of small schools, highlighted by the **Report on the National Education Convention**, are possibly a more restricted curriculum, limitations in available physical resources, difficulty in providing services such as remedial teaching, the professional isolation of teachers, and the disproportionate effect which a persistently under-performing teacher would have on the educational careers of the children in such a school.

School size is not necessarily correlated with effectiveness of provision and teaching. On this point, the **Report** concluded that there is "*not . . . an argument for amalgamating smaller schools into larger units unless the education provided is going to be more effective for the majority of pupils affected*" (p. 35). While acknowledging this important consideration, the **Report** went on to point out, given the rapidly increasing significance of education for the development of society as a whole, that school size and curricular diversity are likely to become more critical factors in educational provision in the future, especially in small towns and rural communities. The **Report** concluded that "*it will become even more critical in the future that [communities] have more effective, more curricular-rich and, therefore, larger schools*" (p. 35).

Educational quality will continue to be the main criterion in considering primary school size, taking into account both the needs of local communities and wider social and cultural factors. Rationalisation of primary school facilities will continue to be critically examined as enrolments fall and before making any significant capital investment.

Historically, primary school accommodation was provided on a parish basis. Demographic trends and population movements, especially in urban areas, suggest that rationalisation and additional accommodation requirements need to be examined on a wider geographical basis than that prescribed by parish boundaries. As a general rule, additional classroom accommodation will not be provided where there is suitable surplus accommodation in an adjoining parish. The commitment to the centrality of the creative and performing arts at primary level will be assisted by commissioning a design brief for new school buildings which will facilitate the development of arts studies.

Structures for Rationalisation

The ***Report on the National Education Convention*** identified the importance of an adequate research and statistical basis for formulating policy on rationalisation. It recorded the view of the Convention Secretariat that *"catchment area studies are needed which would provide detailed information on the present situation in terms of age and condition of schools, distances between schools, demographic projections, unit costs and associated data. Studies on the effectiveness of small schools are also needed"* (p. 36).

It is essential that decisions on school provision, rationalisation and amalgamation be widely perceived to be cost-effective, equitable and reasonable and to be based on a rigorous evaluation of requirements and needs, at both regional and national levels. The sensitivity and complexity of the issues raised require, in each instance, a broadly based agreement that the decision-making process has allowed for proper consultation and has adequately considered all the relevant issues.

The approach to rationalisation will involve co-ordinated action at both national and regional levels.

A commission on school accommodation needs will be established at the earliest opportunity. Its initial task, at primary level, will be to undertake a major study to provide a comprehensive statistical and demographic analysis which will underpin policy formulation on rationalisation. The commission will also recommend criteria and procedures for school provision and planning, taking account of the diversity of needs and plurality within the system, including the effectiveness of small schools. It will provide detailed information on the current and projected positions in relation to school provision. This will facilitate informed debate by all concerned interests and the wider community as an input into final national policy decisions on school provision. Such policy decisions will provide the national framework for the policy development and implementation by each education board within available resources. The commission will operate for a maximum period of five years after which its functions will transfer to the education boards.

The education boards will be responsible, on a continuing basis, for the development and updating of catchment area studies in their regions. This will be part of their statutory obligation to continually evaluate school accommodation needs and the provision of specialist facilities, and to make recommendations to the Minister for Education. Final decisions will be made at national level, based on published criteria related to educational, building and financial factors. The allocation of resources and the determination of national priorities will remain functions of the Minister for Education.

Each education board will introduce arrangements for managing the rationalisation process, in accordance with the national framework for policy development.

Framework for Funding

Expenditure

The Convention Secretariat noted that "*throughout their long history the Irish people have demonstrated a creditable commitment to the value of education and to making sacrifices to attain it and make it available. This has never been more in evidence than in recent decades when the level of investment in education has expanded greatly*" (background paper, **Report** p. 144). Total expenditure, at primary level, increased from £19 million in 1965 to an estimated £718.9 million in 1995. Expenditure per student at first level increased more than threefold in real terms from 1965 to 1995.

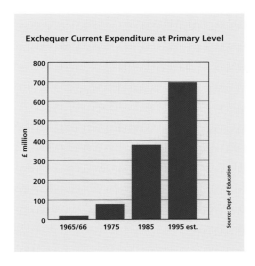

Exchequer Current Expenditure at Primary Level

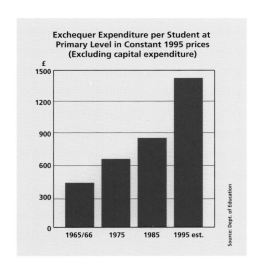

Exchequer Expenditure per Student at Primary Level in Constant 1995 prices (Excluding capital expenditure)

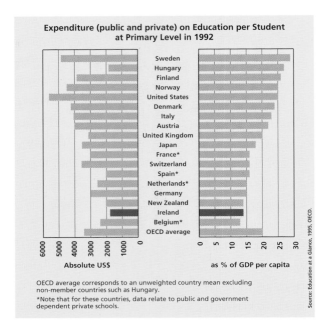

A high proportion of the public funds spent on primary education is non-discretionary. Pay and pensions, mainly of teachers, represent 91 per cent (some £632.6 million) of the estimated current expenditure for primary education (£696.5 million). Existing commitments include pay rates determined centrally through national negotiations, and the commitments in the *Programme for Competitiveness and Work*, including commitments to reducing the pupil-teacher ratio and to the provision of additional remedial teachers.

The number of teachers in the primary system has increased gradually from 14,311 in 1965 to 20,776 in 1993. The pupil-teacher ratio at primary level decreased significantly, from 32:9 to 24.3:1, during the same period.

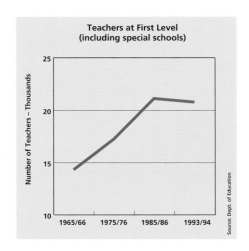

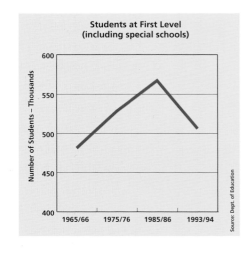

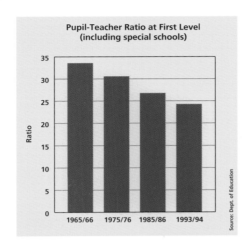

**Pupil-Teacher Ratio at First Level
(including special schools)**

Source: Dept. of Education

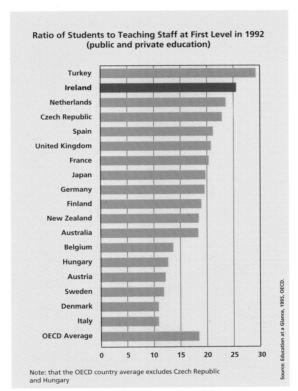

**Ratio of Students to Teaching Staff at First Level in 1992
(public and private education)**

Note: that the OECD country average excludes Czech Republic and Hungary

Source: Education at a Glance, 1995, OECD.

The balance of £63.9 million in the estimates for current primary education relates to the non-pay, non-capital requirements of the education system. In relation to the non-pay element, existing commitments include commitments in the ***Programme for Competitiveness and Work*** and in the ***Government of Renewal*** policy document to increasing concentration on disadvantaged areas.

In the future, the funding of all primary schools will be put on the same basis, with additional funding for schools designated as disadvantaged.

Investment in Primary Education

The education system has a special role to play in Ireland's social and economic development. Future capacity to support national, social and economic infrastructure depends on the productive base of the economy, which in turn depends on the knowledge and skills available within the economy. The economic strengths and resources of society are the source of expenditure on education and, ideally, the return from this expenditure will provide the source of future economic growth and social well-being. Thus, the allocation of resources to education and the distribution of those resources within the education system are crucial issues in the debate on national economic and social prosperity.

The provision of adequate resources for primary education will continue to be a priority. National and international research indicates that primary education is fundamentally important in determining children's life chances. The major demographic changes will increase flexibility and resource options, particularly in relation to allocating additional resources to students with special needs and to disadvantaged areas. It is essential that resources are used effectively and efficiently. For this reason, all programmes will be subject to continuous review and evaluation. In the allocation of resources, priority will be given to students in greatest need.

Benefits derived from primary education are key determinants of the extent to which the individual citizen participates in society: all subsequent education and training are built upon the foundation of primary education. In renewing the Government's commitment to a democratically structured society, the allocation of resources to primary education is both socially and economically essential.

3 Second-Level Education

Introduction

Overall Aim

Building on the foundation of primary education, second-level education aims to provide a comprehensive, high-quality learning environment which enables all students to live full lives, appropriate to their stage of development, and to realise their potential as individuals and as citizens. It aims to prepare students for adult life and to help them proceed to further education or directly to employment.

Educational objectives at this level promote the right of each student to full and equal access, participation and benefit from educational provision, in accordance with her/his ability. Whatever their socio-economic background, gender or special educational needs, individual students are encouraged to reach their full potential as they advance through the education system. The education of each student is valued equally, despite a wide range of individual differences in background, abilities or early experiences and achievements.

Structure

The second-level sector comprises secondary, vocational, community and comprehensive schools. There are just over 370,000 students in this sector, attending a total of 782 publicly aided schools; 461 of these schools are secondary, 248 are vocational and seventy-three are community or comprehensive. In addition, there are thirty-eight other aided and non-aided schools.

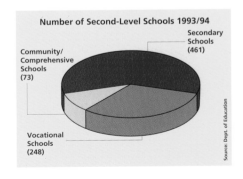

Number of Second-Level Schools 1993/94

Secondary Schools (461)

Community/ Comprehensive Schools (73)

Vocational Schools (248)

Source: Dept. of Education

Secondary schools, educating 61 per cent of second-level students, are privately owned and managed. The majority are conducted by religious communities and the remainder by Boards of Governors or by individuals. Over 95 per cent of the cost of teachers' salaries are met by the State. In addition, allowances and capitation grants are paid to the 95 per cent of secondary schools which participate in the free education scheme. The estimated State support for secondary schools amounted to £397 million in 1994.

Vocational schools, educating 26 per cent of all second-level students, are administered by vocational education committees. Vocational schools are funded up to 93 per cent of the total cost of provision. The balance is provided by receipts generated by the committees.

Community and Comprehensive schools, educating 13 per cent of second-level students, are allocated individual budgets by the State.

Second-level education consists of a three-year junior cycle followed by a two- or three-year senior cycle. The Junior Certificate examination is taken after three years. In senior cycle there is an optional one-year Transition Year Programme followed by a choice of three two-year Leaving Certificate programmes.

Junior Cycle

The junior cycle covers a vital period in young people's lives when they encounter significant changes in their educational experience. The Junior Certificate Programme was introduced in 1989 to provide a single unified programme for students aged broadly between twelve and fifteen years. This programme seeks to extend and deepen the quality of students' educational experience in terms of knowledge, understanding, skills and competencies and to prepare them for further study at senior cycle. The Junior Certificate Programme also contributes to the moral and spiritual development of students, and encourages them to develop qualities of responsible citizenship in a national, European and global context.

Senior Cycle

Increased participation rates at second level have broadened the diversity, abilities and aspirations of students in second-level schools. The challenge of providing an appropriate and beneficial education to all students is considerable: students must be prepared for life in a rapidly changing society while developments in the area of vocational training need to be integrated with general education policy.

One of the main objectives of educational policy is to encourage and facilitate as many students as possible to continue in full-time education after the end of the junior cycle. **A major objective will be that the percentage of the sixteen-to-eighteen-year-old age-group completing senior cycle will increase to at least 90 per cent by the year 2000.**

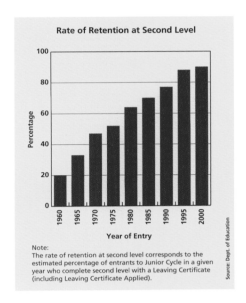

Rate of Retention at Second Level

Year of Entry

Source: Dept. of Education

Note:
The rate of retention at second level corresponds to the estimated percentage of entrants to Junior Cycle in a given year who complete second level with a Leaving Certificate (including Leaving Certificate Applied).

This objective will be achieved through providing a combination of an effective foundation of general education and a strengthened and expanded vocational orientation. The availability of the option of a three-year senior cycle for all students entering second-level education from 1994 onwards presents new possibilities for achieving the objective.

Curriculum

Key Principles

Breadth, balance and coherence will underpin curricular development at second level. Breadth involves the provision of a wide range of different experiences which nurture holistic development. Balance establishes appropriate relationships among the diverse aspects of the curriculum. Coherence provides students with broad and balanced programmes at the appropriate depth, while also encouraging students to make connections between the varying facets of their educational experiences.

Transition – Primary to Second Level

Transitional Challenges

The change from primary to second level affects students in different ways. Some thrive on the difference. For others, problems in making the change can affect them adversely throughout their time at second level. Such problems arise from:

- poor communications between primary and second-level schools

- difficulty for some students in gaining access to the first-choice school

- differences in teaching methods and approaches

- curricula which do not suit a student's particular abilities and aspirations

- being compelled to make subject choices, or choice of subject level, too soon and later facing unduly restrictive options.

Actions

Junior cycle education, involving co-operation and not competition among schools, will be open to all on the basis of equal opportunity and equality of participation, including gender equality and equality for those with special needs. **Responsibility for the realisation of this objective will be assigned statutorily to the education boards**. In observing the statutory objective, education boards will be responsible for the implementation and review of admissions policies to second-level schools, so as to ensure that national agreements and policies on selective academic entry tests are operated.

Access to a more student-centred curriculum will be facilitated initially on entry to junior cycle. For instance, the National Council for Curriculum and Assessment will be asked to ensure that the study of modern languages, with an increased emphasis on oral/aural components will build on the European Awareness Programme at primary level. Similarly, the courses in science will be planned as an extension of the science component of the primary social and environmental programme. Furthermore, creative and performing arts courses will relate to the arts methodology at primary level. Thus, these courses can play a significant role in facilitating the transition from primary to second level.

An important principle in regard to transition is that the students will be able to participate and gain experience in the widest possible range of activities and subject areas during the first year. Such a broad initial foundation, for at least the first year of junior cycle, will be the basis of student development subsequently within the framework of the Junior Certificate. In this way, the curriculum at junior cycle can be more purposefully tailored to meet the needs, abilities and interests of individual students. In addition, students, parents and schools should be able to make more realistic and informed decisions relating to future study and the achievement of optimum progress for each student. Since it is recognised that students mature at different rates, **they should be allowed maximum choice for as long as possible before making decisions regarding examination subject choice or subject level**.

The education boards will also be responsible for ensuring that arrangements are in place for the effective tracking and monitoring of the school attendance of students of compulsory school-going age. One aspect of this responsibility will be ensuring the transfer of students' profile cards from primary to second-level schools. Any information on a profile card should not prejudice a student on entry to a second-level school. Parents will have the right of access to these profile cards and other student assessment records in the context of developing strong and meaningful home-school links. The objective in making this information available is to assist in the process of identifying the student's learning and other needs.

Junior Cycle

Curricular Aims/Principles

The primary objective of the junior cycle is for students to complete a broad, balanced and coherent course of study in a variety of curricular areas relevant to their own personal development and to allow them to achieve a level of competence in these which will enable them to proceed to senior cycle education.

The introduction of the Junior Certificate programme in 1989 provided a single, unified programme for students. The Junior Certificate programme is based on the following curricular principles:

- *breadth and balance*: every student should have a wide range of educational experiences and particular attention should be given to reinforcing and developing the skills of numeracy, literacy and spoken language

- *relevance*: the curriculum should provide for the immediate and future needs of the student in the context of the cultural, economic and social environment and promote equality of participation and benefit between girls and boys

- *quality*: every student should be challenged to achieve the highest possible standards of excellence, having regard to their different aptitudes and abilities

- *continuity and progression*: education should be seen as a continuum, with close links between the curriculum, learning processes and teaching methods at primary level and at second level, in the junior cycle

- *coherence*: the curriculum should provide a coherent and consistent educational experience for students through a broad and balanced programme with appropriate depth of treatment, while encouraging students to make connections between the different aspects of their educational experience.

Curricular Framework

The junior cycle curriculum has a wider perspective than the mere choice and range of subjects. The curricular framework at junior cycle is intended to provide a wide educational context for the various subjects on offer. It will ensure a smoother transition from primary to second level and from junior cycle to senior cycle, recognising that a young person's progress does not proceed uniformly or at an even pace. The objective will be that, on completion of the junior cycle, all students, in accordance with their abilities and aptitudes, will have achieved or experienced the following:

- competence in literacy, numeracy and spoken language skills which will allow them to participate as young adults in society

- experience in various areas of activity – artistic, intellectual, scientific, physical and practical

- formative experiences in moral, religious and spiritual education

- knowledge and supportive guidance in matters of personal health, sexual awareness and relationships

- competence and understanding in practical skills, including computer literacy and information technology

- knowledge and appreciation of their social, cultural and physical heritage and environment

- understanding and appreciation of the central concepts of citizenship.

The effectiveness with which the curriculum is implemented will be evaluated on the basis of these objectives. Setting such objectives will enable schools to plan and implement cross-curricular activities and to make specific interventions designed to address particular needs.

The creative and performing arts are distinctive and intrinsically valuable educational disciplines. The new junior cycle curriculum regards arts and culture as key elements within the school experience of young people. The provision of arts education is an issue of social equality and there is an increasing recognition that cultural poverty is a significant part of disadvantage. The creative and performing arts have an important role as part of the whole school curriculum. They can be a key contributor to the school ethos and to its place in the local community. They provide occasions where students, teachers and parents can work together in a mutually reinforcing way. It is important, therefore, that all schools develop a strong arts and cultural policy and identity.

Scientific and technological developments have an enormous influence on our society, whether through their economic and social effects or though their impact on individual lifestyle. In a fast-changing world, it is important that people are able to understand such innovations and to evaluate their implications. Apart from their wider effects, science and technology play an important role in the student's intellectual formation, complementing educational experiences in the arts and humanities.

In view of the demands on young people of an increasingly sophisticated and technological environment, it is important that all students should receive a foundation in science and technology, augmenting the new science programme which will form an integral part of the review of social and environmental programme at primary level. Either science or a technological subject will, therefore, form part of the core programme for each student in junior cycle.

Each school will be expected to provide students with experience in the following areas, as recommended by the National Council for Curriculum and Assessment: Language and Literature, Mathematical Studies, Science and

Technology, Civic, Social and Political Education, Arts Education, Religious Education, Guidance, Counselling and Pastoral Care, Physical Education, Health Education including Personal and Social Development, Relationships and Sexuality Education.

While some of these may be provided through the formal timetabling of courses such as Irish, English and Mathematics, other areas such as guidance, health education, relationships and sexuality education may best be provided either on a cross-curricular approach or by specific short courses, classes, modules or other interventions at various times throughout the junior cycle. Each school will be required to involve management, parents and staff in developing and making available its policy on Relationships and Sexuality Education.

The curricular framework will apply to all second-level schools and to all students in the junior cycle. For the purposes of certification, the following specific requirements will be necessary. The programme for all students at junior cycle will include a core of Irish, English, Mathematics, a science or a technological subject, and at least three further subjects from a wide range of full courses and short courses. **All students should have access to the study of a modern European language and to a recognised full course in at least one creative or performing art form**.

Modules and short courses on a variety of subject areas will be developed and introduced gradually to Junior Certificate students, with some consequent adjustments to the list of required subject courses. A combination of full and short courses could meet the curricular principles of breadth and balance. This approach underlines the greater flexibility with which schools will be able to adapt the curriculum to the specific needs, abilities and interests of individual students.

Continuity in the teaching of Irish is important between primary and second-level education. The aim is to build on the knowledge and skills developed during the primary years, allowing the students to acquire such competence as will enable them to achieve success and satisfaction in learning Irish.

Similarly, continuity will be fostered between the social and environmental programme at primary level and science and technology at second level, and between the broadly based creative and performing arts curriculum at primary level and the arts curriculum at second level. The National Council for Curriculum and Assessment will be asked to develop recognised full Junior Certificate courses in drama and dance to assist this continuity.

To cater for differences in students' abilities and aptitudes, all subjects are now offered at higher and ordinary levels. Irish, English and Mathematics are also offered at foundation level. **Students should be encouraged to follow courses at the highest level indicated by their capacity, thus challenging them to develop their potential and secure their access to courses appropriate to their ability at senior cycle**.

Senior Cycle

Aims

The aims of the senior cycle are to encourage and facilitate students to continue in full-time education during the post-compulsory period by providing a stimulating range of programmes suited to their abilities, aptitudes and interests. The objectives are to develop each student's potential to the full, and equip them for work or further education.

Context

The restructuring of the senior cycle has been influenced by a number of factors. For the vast majority of students, the Junior Certificate is no longer the final examination. Completion rates to the end of senior cycle have increased dramatically over the last thirty years to over 77 per cent at present. The target is for at least a 90 per cent completion rate by the end of the 1990s. The traditional Leaving Certificate programme does not cater adequately for the variety of needs and abilities of students now completing senior cycle. A fundamental objective of the restructuring of the senior cycle is to cater more effectively for the needs and aptitudes of all students. Particular attention will be paid to ensuring gender equality in and through the senior cycle and to the needs of students who are disadvantaged by socio-economic circumstances and by physical or mental handicap.

Students may now spend up to three years in senior cycle. They may follow a two-year Leaving Certificate programme immediately after Junior Certificate, or they may opt to follow a Transition Year programme before a two-year Leaving Certificate.

The Leaving Certificate is structured as a two-year programme. The Transition Year has been introduced to provide students with enriched opportunities for personal development. Accordingly, schools are not permitted to offer a three-year Leaving Certificate programme, since this would undermine the Transition Year objectives.

A major restructuring of the senior cycle is under way, involving four main elements:

- the availability of the Transition Year Programme as an option for all second-level schools
- the revision of the established Leaving Certificate Programme
- the introduction of a new Leaving Certificate Applied course
- the development and expansion of the Leaving Certificate Vocational Programme.

An important overall objective of the restructuring of the senior cycle is to provide for the holistic development of all students progressing to the end of senior cycle and to foster the sense of self-esteem, self-reliance and innovation which will empower them to actively shape the social and economic future of society.

Transition Year Programme

The Transition Year Programme is interdisciplinary and student-centred. By freeing students to take responsibility for their own learning, the programme helps them to learn skills and to evaluate life in ways and in situations which arise outside the boundaries of the certificate programmes. The ***Report on the National Education Convention*** recorded the Convention's participants' enthusiasm for the Transition Year option: "*students matured during the year and sometimes revised their subject and career choices*" (p. 75).

Within the challenging framework of the Transition Year Programme, teachers gain greater flexibility and professional opportunities to design curricula, modules and short courses which are specially tailored to the specific needs of their students. The school is enriched by a range of active learning methods. Parents, the community and local enterprise can bring to the Transition Year a sense of the world and so contribute to an education which faces the demands and pleasures of life, work, sport and leisure.

The Transition Year offers a special opportunity to enjoyably underpin, in a non-examination environment, the importance of the Irish language and culture, the prospects of our European and world environment, the wealth of creative and performing arts activity and heritage and the equality of women and men in society.

Leaving Certificate Framework

Students, parents and employers accord a high social status to the Leaving Certificate. Policy, therefore, will be to build upon and expand programmes within the Leaving Certificate framework.

Development will be based on a number of considerations: the provision of a broadly based general education up to the end of senior cycle; the preservation of the best elements of existing programmes; an increased emphasis on the vocational orientation of all subjects; reinforcing the artistic dimension of the curriculum; the fostering of a strong sense of cultural identity through the promotion of the Irish language and Irish literature; and the development of an active appreciation of the European dimension in and through education.

The new Leaving Certificate structure, with its three separate orientations – the established Leaving Certificate Programme, the Leaving Certificate Applied and the Leaving Certificate Vocational Programme – provides a coherent framework to broaden the scope of educational provision at senior cycle and to facilitate schools to provide the most appropriate senior-cycle programme for all their students.

In order to provide a comprehensive range of senior-cycle programmes, close co-operation between schools in a given locality will be necessary, where rationalisation is not an appropriate option. The education boards will be responsible for ensuring that appropriate arrangements are put in place to provide a variety of senior-cycle programmes in a locality. Special consideration in the provision of resources will be given to small schools in isolated areas.

Programmes at senior cycle will be characterised by continuity with and progression from junior cycle, with an appropriate balance between personal and social development, vocational studies and preparation for work and for further education. The respective weighting among these elements will vary according to the programme.

Established Leaving Certificate Programme

The majority of senior-cycle students will continue to choose the Leaving Certificate Programme. Syllabi are being reviewed and updated on a phased basis by the National Council for Curriculum and Assessment and the first six revised syllabi will be introduced in September 1995.

Leaving Certificate Applied

The **Report on the National Education Convention** recorded that "*the need for an alternative to present provision at Leaving Certificate was universally accepted*" (p. 76). A separate and distinct form of Leaving Certificate known as the Leaving Certificate Applied is currently being developed. This Leaving Certificate programme will allow for an extension of the active learning approaches developed in the Transition Year Programme and for links to further vocational training.

It is essential that the talents of all students are recognised and that they are afforded an opportunity to develop responsibility, self-esteem and self-knowledge. The fundamental goal of the Leaving Certificate Applied is to prepare students for the transition from school to adult and working life, including further education. Scientific and technological subjects and the creative and performing arts have an intrinsic value and they complement each other. The integrated nature of the curriculum in the Leaving Certificate Applied allows expression of these intrinsic and complementary values.

In an age when scientific and technological developments have such an enormous influence on work, it is important that people are able to understand such innovations and to evaluate their implications. Similarly, increased links with Europe mean that oral competence in modern European languages should be fostered and encouraged, while in an age of satellite broadcasting and mass cultural industries, students should be encouraged to become makers and critical receivers rather than passive consumers of a mass culture.

This programme will focus on the needs and interests of students using a variety of methodologies, making maximum use of local resources and paying particular attention to involvement of the local community. Thus, the programme will not be just a school-based programme, but will have an important community dimension.

While certification in the Leaving Certificate Applied will not be a qualification for direct entry to third-level courses, students who successfully complete the programme will be able to proceed to many Post-Leaving-Certificate courses.

To support this process, the Leaving Certificate Applied will be fully integrated into the system for a certification of educational and training qualifications being developed by TEASTAS – the Irish National Certification Authority (see Chapter 4).

The Leaving Certificate Applied will be introduced on a phased basis from September 1995.

Leaving Certificate Vocational Programme

This two-year programme is based on combinations of Leaving Certificate subjects at higher, ordinary or foundation levels and affords students full opportunity for access to third-level education. The programme's objective is to strengthen and expand the vocational dimension of the learning experiences offered to students in the senior cycle. It offers equal accessibility to both girls and boys. Modern European languages are an integral part of the programme.

A central focus of the programme is to foster a spirit of innovation and initiative in young people by developing vocational, technological, communicative and interpersonal skills within the same programme. In addition, the revised Leaving Certificate Vocational Programme requires students to follow three link modules – *Enterprise Education, Preparation for Work* and *Work Experience*.

The purpose of the link modules is to develop young peoples' creative and innovative capacities by offering an opportunity to develop their own ideas, put them into practice and evaluate the results. By so doing it seeks to foster the skills and attributes which assist young people to be successful as employees or to become entrepreneurs and employers in their own right. To achieve this, the link modules are activity-driven. Creative and innovative skills are fostered through involvement in activity-based learning. Activities in the form of projects, mini-enterprises, visits to workplaces, interchange with employers and report writing are central to the implementation of the link modules.

The revised Leaving Certificate Vocational Programme is being introduced on a phased basis and the programme will be implemented in full by September 1996.

Evaluation of Standards

It is particularly important for students, society and the economy that the standards in Leaving Certificate subjects compare favourably with the highest international benchmarks. A specific responsibility of the Department's inspectorate will be to carry out each year a full evaluation of the standards achieved in specific subjects in the Leaving Certificate by comparison with the highest standards in a representative sample of developed countries. For the purposes of this evaluation the inspectors will be joined by experts from overseas, who will have expertise in, and access to data for, the comparator countries. The objective will be that one or two subjects will be scrutinised each year, with the overall aim that all Leaving Certificate subjects will be fully examined over a ten-year cycle. The reports of the evaluation group will be published. They could also be usefully debated in the Dáil.

Students with Special Needs

Context

The principles set out in relation to catering for special needs at the primary level will continue to be applied, as appropriate, to students in second-level education. As in the primary sector, the objective will be to ensure a continuum of provision for special educational needs, ranging from occasional help within the ordinary school to full-time education in a dedicated centre or unit, with students being enabled to move from one type of provision to another as necessary and practicable.

Action

At present, five second-level schools in Dublin and Cork are recognised as designated schools for students with physical, visual or hearing impairment and they have been given additional teachers and support personnel. Most of these students can be included in normal classes for most of the curriculum and they sit the public examinations, some with special concessions. The Special Education Review Committee concluded that, "*By and large, this model of provision works well and enables the student with a disability to benefit to the greatest extent possible from attendance in an ordinary school. It is a model which could usefully be extended to other areas of the country*" (**Report of Special Education Review Committee**, pp. 65-66) In the future, each education board will be responsible for designating ordinary second-level schools to meet the range of special needs of students in its region. Building on the examples in Dublin and Cork, these schools will have classes dedicated to meet particular needs as well as access to specialist expertise and facilities, in addition to providing the full second-level curriculum.

Each education board will have a statutory responsibility for all students in its region who have been registered as having special needs and will co-ordinate provision for them, including support services.

As in the case of primary schools, existing special schools will fulfil an expanded role as schools dealing with a variety of special needs and as regional resource centres. Each student with special needs will be assigned, as necessary and appropriate, to the nearest appropriate special school in the region, whether or not s/he attends the school. If it is agreed that the student will attend an ordinary school, s/he and her/his parents will still have access to the support services available in the special school. The decision-making process, in relation to the placement of a student in an ordinary and/or a special school, will be a collaborative one, made by the parents and professionals involved, with the objective of providing what is best suited to the child's development and needs.

In the case of the small minority of students with significant learning difficulties, where special provision is required, **the education board will make arrangements for the writing of a statement of special educational needs for these students on an individual basis**. The statement will identify the nature of these needs, the special educational provision required to meet them, and the school in which they can be most effectively met.

More generally, it will be the responsibility of each school to present, in its school plan, its policy on the assessment of students. This will include a section on the identification of students with special needs and on how the school proposes, with the co-operation of parents, to help them. The main focus of the assessment procedure will be to identify the student's potential. The identification of special needs should be a collective responsibility of all the relevant subject teachers, having collaboratively considered the student's needs, informed and supported by the special/ professional support services. This procedure could be co-ordinated, for example, by the principal, year head or pastoral care teacher.

The School Psychological service will be progressively expanded to ensure that every student with learning and behavioural difficulties has access to help at the earliest possible stage. Each education board will be responsible for ensuring the co-ordination of the School Psychological service in its area. In addition, each education board will liaise closely with the relevant health board in relation to the school health service and the clinic-based assessment services in its area.

The Special Education Review Committee has made detailed recommendations on meeting the needs of students with particular disabilities. A special task force has been set up within the Department of Education to implement the report's findings, within the constraints of available resources.

A major focus of policy in tackling disadvantage will be to ensure continuity and consistency of interventions in support of educationally disadvantaged students throughout their educational lives. Specifically, this will include, as recommended in the ***Report on the National Education Convention***, more co-operation between primary schools that are designated as disadvantaged and the second-level schools to which the students of these schools transfer. The phased expansion of the Home-School Links Scheme will continue. While resources will continue to be allocated to schools designated as disadvantaged for this purpose, all schools will be required to have a formal Home-School Links policy as part of their school plan. In addition, targeted support interventions will be continued in order to assist schools catering for students with special needs through, for example, the provision of guidance counsellors, remedial teachers and other specialist support services.

Curricular Initiatives

Junior Cycle Schools Programme

Aimed at the objective 'equality of participation', this programme, which is at an advanced stage of development by the National Council for Curriculum and Assessment, is designed to reach out more effectively to a small but important minority of students whose particular needs are not addressed adequately in the present, broadly based Junior Certificate.

The Schools Programme will be specifically aimed at:

- students who show clear signs of not coping with the volume and complexity of the present mainstream curriculum

- students who are underachieving significantly in literacy and numeracy

- students whose attendance and/or behaviour and attitudinal patterns indicate a marked degree of alienation from school

- students who have specific disabilities which preclude them from participating in regular courses

- students whose social and cultural environment does not equip them for the requirements of the normal Junior Certificate programme.

Although, these objectives will be specified in a national curriculum framework, there will be enough flexibility for schools to accommodate the particular needs and abilities of their own students.

The Junior Cycle Schools Programme will emphasise the essential skills of numeracy and literacy as well as personal and social needs. All students will work towards Junior Certificate Foundation Level in English and Mathematics as a minimum, and will study a relevant course in Irish language and culture. Students will also be encouraged and facilitated to take other Junior Certificate syllabi to examination stage.

Youthreach

The education sector and FÁS are involved in the delivery of Youthreach programmes. Youthreach is intended for early school leavers, aged fifteen to eighteen. Basic skills training, practical work training and general education are major features of the programme. The application of new technology is integrated into all aspects of the programme. The objective of these measures is to equip early school-leavers with the skills needed for employment or further training and to provide integrated education, training and work experience over a two-year period and thereby to enhance their job prospects and life chances.

A National Foundation Certificate programme is being developed for students who complete the Foundation Phase of the programme. Access to the Leaving Certificate Applied and other appropriate courses will be facilitated after this phase.

Curriculum Development Projects

The National Council for Curriculum and Assessment will set up curriculum development projects for students who have special educational needs. To accommodate educational provisions for students with disabilities in mainstream schools, curriculum review will allow for flexibility, addition and adaptation. Where necessary, students with disabilities in mainstream settings will be provided with adapted teaching methods, materials and curricula. The curricular needs of all students in specialist settings will be reviewed, based on ages, abilities, needs and aspirations. Appropriate in-career development will be arranged for teachers of students who have special needs.

General Reform

As well as taking special initiatives, the revised curricula in Junior and Senior Cycle are designed to give second-level provision the capability with which to deal with the wide spread of students and abilities and the flexibility to meet the particular special needs of individuals.

Children of the Travelling Community

Approach to Policy

The participation of traveller children in second-level schools is very low. The main aim for children over the age of twelve in the traveller community is to encourage them to continue in full-time education and to promote the continuation of their full inclusive participation in education, while retaining respect and value for their distinctive culture. All educational institutions, which are in receipt of public funding, have a responsibility to provide for travellers who wish to attend them. Traveller children have the same rights as all other children to have access to publicly funded institutions.

The **Report on the National Education Convention** concluded, in regard to traveller children, that *"their participation rates at all levels of the education system are unacceptably low for a democratic society"* (p. 127). Many young travellers have received their education in special classes at primary level or in Junior Training Centres at second level. The excellent work of these classes and centres has been recognised. They will now be reorganised under the aegis of the education boards. The education boards will facilitate the establishment of links with adjacent schools. One of the main functions of the Training Centres will be to provide transitional classes with the aim of integrating traveller students in mainstream classes. Second-level schools will adapt their curriculum, as appropriate, to provide a starting point for advancement to senior cycle courses. The purpose of this is to ensure that the education provided matches the student's special needs and abilities, while at the same time providing access to the wide diversity of experience that a second-level school can offer its students. The Special Education Review Committee concluded, in relation to traveller children, that *"insofar as possible, they should be* *educated together with their peers from the settled community and not in segregated groups*" (**Report**, p. 158).

The overall policy objective is that, within ten years, all traveller children of second-level, school-going age will complete junior cycle education and 50 per cent will complete the senior cycle. The education boards will have the specific responsibility for achieving this objective in their regions. The achievement of this objective will be supported by:

- the inclusion in schools' plans of an admissions policy in relation to travellers, in accordance with national and regional guidelines

- the education boards putting in place induction programmes involving the family, the primary school where the student is enrolled, and the second-level school to which s/he is about to transfer

- the provision of modules on travellers and traveller culture in pre-service and in-career development of teachers

- the continuing development by the National Council for Curriculum and Assessment of appropriate curriculum and assessment procedures to meet the special needs of traveller children, including the provision of appropriate texts and materials

- the continuing development of the visiting teacher service

- comprehensive and regularly updated surveys of traveller education

- the monitoring of school attendance patterns.

Teaching Methods

Strategy for Development

Revision of the curriculum needs to be supported by changes in teaching methods. The development of teaching methodology seeks to ensure that the methods used are appropriate to the objectives sought. Teaching methods employed are central to the process of innovation and change.

Traditional didactic teaching methods delivered knowledge and information from teacher to student. "*The need for styles of pedagogy which engage and involve all students more actively in the teaching-learning interaction than was traditional*" was emphasised in the **Report on the National Education Convention** (p. 73). The importance of complementing traditional methods with a wider range of teaching strategies is a key element in realising the objectives of the restructured second-level curriculum. New strategies will also help to harmonise approaches between primary and second-level schools.

An important aim in relation to teaching methodology will be the continued **development of whole-school approaches**, involving the body of teachers in a school. This partnership will result in greater flexibility, openness and innovation since it will be concerned with the principles of sharing, supporting and teamwork and will facilitate the creation of a learning environment appropriate to each particular school. By pooling their expertise teachers can contribute very significantly to the quality of education of all students.

Key elements in the promotion of new approaches will be appropriate changes in pre-service education and a comprehensive programme of in-career development in the context of the very significant resources now available for this purpose. In-career programmes will build upon the needs identified by the schools, arising from each school's internal evaluation and planning processes (see Chapter 8).

Assessment

Objectives

Careful assessment underpins all good educational practice. Assessment also contributes to securing continuity of provision in the progression from one stage of education to the next. The skills and procedures for affirming successes and diagnosing difficulties are fundamental to the teacher's work and vital to the learner's progress.

Assessment at second level encompasses a range of related processes used to support the personal, educational and vocational guidance of students towards the realisation of their full potential.

Assessment encompasses all the methods used to evaluate the achievements of an individual or group. It is usually concerned with the gathering of information related to the students' knowledge, understanding, skills and aptitudes. Assessment procedures range from the formal, such as written examinations, to the informal, such as the teacher's observation. Continuous assessment, which may be described as formative assessment, is an integral part of teaching and is something which every teacher undertakes. Summative assessment is carried out at the end of the year or course and normally takes the form of a test or examination.

Assessment, and the uses to which it is put, influence teaching methods and the wider school environment. Assessment procedures should be comprehensive enough to test the full range of abilities across the curriculum and to evaluate all the elements of learning. The National Council for Curriculum and Assessment has reported to the Minister for Education that a change in the examination system, even to a modest degree, would bring substantial improvements to the teaching and learning process and to the quality of the educational outcomes in schools.

It is particularly important that assessment methods should fully support the achievement of the full range of curricular objectives in the new Junior Certificate programme. It is equally important that assessment methods promote and support the more diversified range of teaching approaches necessary to achieve those objectives. For this purpose, a special Implementation Group will be established within three months of the publication of the White Paper. The Group will be representative of the concerned interests and relevant independent experts. It will be chaired by a senior official in the Department of Education. The mandate of the Group will be to draw up a detailed timetable and programme for a fundamental restructuring of the assessment carried out at the end of junior cycle, in order to ensure that the full range of curricular objectives are evaluated, including a very increased role for school-based assessment.

The Leaving Certificate will continue to provide certification of achievement and will be a basis for progression to employment and further education.

The Development of Assessment

The *Report on the National Education Convention* stated that: "*It is the view of the Secretariat that the present system of assessment at Junior Cycle is inadequate and unless reforms are introduced the objectives of the Junior Certificate programme will not be achieved*" (p. 74).

Meeting the objectives of the curriculum at junior cycle requires comprehensive guidelines relating to the various methods of assessment. **An essential shift in emphasis from external examinations to internal assessment will be implemented in the future**. New assessment methods will include projects, orals, aurals and practical work.

Assessment criteria for senior cycle will be developed and broadened from the junior cycle, involving a balance between internal assessment and external examinations. Where internal assessments apply, external scrutiny of such assessments will be ensured.

While external examinations will continue to be the main instrument for assessing achievement at the senior cycle, a wider range of assessment techniques will be necessary. The techniques will evaluate the range of skills that are now demanded in a modern society, including thinking and innovation skills, practical skills and research and problem-solving skills, as well as the ability to apply knowledge.

The modes and techniques of assessment for the Leaving Certificate at higher, ordinary and foundation levels will be consistent with the objectives of the syllabi in so far as this is feasible. **Decisions will be taken on the modes of assessment before any revised syllabi or programmes are introduced in schools**. As the revised syllabi in Leaving Certificate subjects are introduced, the supporting assessment objectives will be set out. The National Council for Curriculum and Assessment will advise the Minister as regards details of assessment and certification arrangements for the Leaving Certificate Applied and for the link and other modules in the Leaving Certificate Vocational Programme. The implications of extending the current range of assessment techniques will be identified and addressed, including necessary pre-service education and in-career development. Any changes will be introduced on a planned basis so that the changes will have the full support and confidence of students, parents, teachers and the wider community.

The current practice of publishing results at national level will continue. However, the Department of Education will not make available publicly the results of individual schools. A part of the whole-school inspection process will include an evaluation of the levels of attainment by students at various ages, by referring to their level of attainment on entry to the school.

Language Assessment

There is a need to further develop oral and aural competence in the Irish Language, and in modern European languages, in second-level schools. To serve this need, there will be a phased increase in the proportion of marks awarded for oral and aural competence in both Irish and modern European languages in the Junior Certificate and Leaving Certificate examinations. The policy objective will be to move towards a position where 60 per cent of the total marks available will be awarded for oral and aural competence in the Irish language and in modern European languages. The objective, and its implementation, will be the subject of full consultation with the National Council for Curriculum and Assessment. Furthermore, second-level schools will be encouraged to promote a wide range of languages, including Spanish and German.

Time in School

Research findings indicate that the amount of time spent by students in organised learning activities has a critical bearing on their academic performance and all-round development. The total time spent by students in school depends on the length of the school day, the length of the school year and the number of years spent in school.

Second-Level School Year

At second level, the rule requiring 179 days attendance results in 167 days of teaching, when the period of twelve days for the Certificate Examinations has been deducted. In practice, this allowance of twelve days is availed of by all students and teachers, even though less than half the students and a small proportion of teachers are actually involved in the public examinations. In addition, as at primary level, a variety of other factors – such as early closures, special closures, and days when only part of the student body is present in school – have further eroded the required minimum number of teaching days.

In order to ensure the integrity of the school year and the school day, **the Department of Education will issue a circular to all second-level schools, clarifying the relevant, current rules on the basis of the following model**:

Days		
School in operation for teaching		179
(Less 12 days in the case of Certificate Examination students)		
Standard number of closings:		
(a) Saturdays and Sundays	104	
(b) Permitted vacation days	60	
(c) Public and religious holidays	16	
	180	180
Remaining days		6
		365

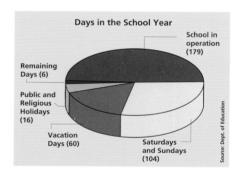

Days in the School Year

An Approach to Policy

Boards of management will be obliged by statute to ensure that schools adhere to the prescribed minimum number of teaching days per annum and to the minimum number of teaching hours per day. The minimum numbers will be prescribed from time to time by the Minister.

In the context of the present minimum, the six "remaining days" will be used for school-related activities, such as curriculum development, school planning and staff development, as well as for special closures.

It is desirable that the period of the Certificate Examinations be used for purposes such as in-career development and in-house examinations and assessment, for students not directly involved in the Certificate Examinations. Discussions will take place with the relevant interests before this proposal is implemented.

Each board of management should critically assess proposals for the closure of its school, in order to determine whether the closure is in the best interests of the students. The boards should bear in mind that the reasons which might warrant the closure of a school for student-teaching purposes need not necessarily justify the non-attendance of teaching staff to engage in other essential or desirable school activities. Each board, therefore, should ensure that the teaching staff, working together to further the aims of the school, avails of the opportunities offered by such closures. Each board should also give parents at the beginning of each year a calendar of events in the school, including closures.

School-Leaving Age

At present, the compulsory school leaving age is fifteen. In future, the school-leaving age will be sixteen or the completion of three years of junior cycle education, whichever is later.

Providing for Schooling

Diversity of Schooling Provision

Second-level education is provided in secondary schools and vocational schools, including community colleges, comprehensive schools and community schools.

The Government is committed to maintaining the diversity of school types, recognising the pluralism of Irish society and the rights of parents to provide for their children's education in schools of their choice, subject to curricular and financial constraints.

New School Buildings

Each education board will be responsible for the identification of the school accommodation needs in its region, taking account of the wishes of parents and the wider community. **In future, education boards will own new school buildings and property and will lease them to different groups of patrons and trustees, in order to provide for the educational needs of their particular area.** This is in line with the practice in other member states of the European Union of providing publicly owned buildings for compulsory education. The ***Report on the National Education Convention*** noted that "*Ireland was seen as unique in requiring citizens to provide privately owned accommodation for this purpose*" (p. 31). These leasing arrangements will be made in accordance with national guidelines and will be subject to the Minister's approval. All buildings for new schools will be provided in this way.

All-Irish Provision

Provision will continue to be made for second-level education through Irish where demand exists and when feasible. **The education boards will have a specific responsibility to identify needs and ensure appropriate provision**. School size determines to a significant extent the range of choice of subjects and levels which can be offered. Consequently, viability may depend on an adequate number of feeder all-Irish primary schools in the catchment area. Education boards will consider various options, including an all-Irish unit within an existing school, where a separate school is not a viable option.

Rationalisation

An extensive school building programme was initiated to accommodate the increasing numbers at second level following the introduction of free second-level education in 1967 and the raising of the compulsory schooling age from fourteen to fifteen. To provide a wider range of curriculum options, a new type of comprehensive/community school was introduced and a school rationalisation programme was implemented. As a result, in the period from 1975 to 1993 the number of schools with an enrolment of under 500 decreased from 696 to 448, whereas schools with enrolment of over 500 increased by 186 to 320.

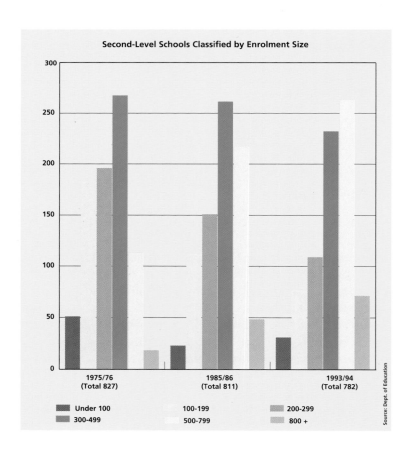

64

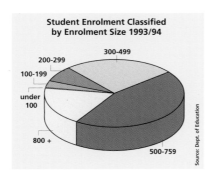

Total enrolment at second level is expected to rise from 367,700 in 1993/94 to a peak of 383,000 in 1997/98 and then to fall back to 376,000 by the year 2000/01 and to 345,000 by 2005/06. Already, the intake to the junior cycle has begun to decline. The policy response to this decline has to take account of likely local and regional variations in these national trends.

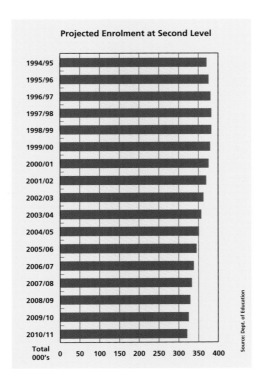

Policy Considerations

The need to offer a broader range of curricular choices and options has been discussed. Its necessity arises from a wider spread of abilities among those participating in second-level education and because of the perceived need to prepare students more fully for life and work in a rapidly changing world. The demand for more extensive and differentiated curricula is emphasised further by the recent expansion of vocational/technical education at senior cycle, in Post-Leaving-Certificate courses and in both adult and continuing education.

The breadth of curriculum required for those students is difficult to achieve in small schools because of the many options and activities which must be made available. At any rate, most small schools are within multi-school catchment areas and it is clearly inefficient to multiply costly additional curricular provision in schools which cater for the same community.

However, school size does not necessarily correlate with effectiveness of provision and teaching across the whole ability and curricular range. The argument for amalgamating small schools into larger units is not sustainable, as the ***Report on the National Education Convention*** noted, *"unless the quality of education provided is going to be more effective for the majority of students"* (p. 35). Nevertheless, given more effective quality of education, school size and curricular diversity are likely to become increasingly critical factors in future educational provision, as education becomes ever more significant for the development of society as a whole. This is especially the case in small towns and rural communities. These extensive considerations led the ***Report*** to conclude that *"it will become even more critical in the future that [communities] have effective, more curricular-rich and, therefore, larger schools"* (p. 35).

Twenty per cent of second-level schools have less than 250 students and only 7 per cent of second-level students attend those schools. Although small schools can be effective, the ***Report on the National Education Convention*** noted that *"small schools of less than 250 pupils with, say, ten to twelve teachers, are necessarily limited in their curricular possibilities, so, if the curriculum options are to be extended (to them), it appears to be a very difficult and expensive task . . . (making) amalgamation pressures appear much less resistible than in primary schools"* (p. 37).

Actions

The policy objective will be to provide second-level schools that are large enough to adequately meet the variety of curricular demands, to meet community education needs and to enhance the role of schools in vocational education and training and adult and continuing education. The rationalisation of second-level facilities will continue to involve consultation with all the interests concerned.

Rationalisation will seek to provide single-campus schools, but when that is not feasible, single multi-campus schools will be considered. Inter-school co-operation will be encouraged in such cases so as to enhance the range of options available to students.

The strengthening of vocational and practical elements at second level and the development of Post-Leaving-Certificate courses will give specialist equipment and accommodation an increasing importance. The full range of facilities and programmes cannot be provided in each individual school, particularly where rationalisation has not been achieved. In these circumstances, education boards will co-ordinate such facilities where necessary. The commitment to the centrality of the creative and performing arts at second level will be assisted by commissioning a design brief for new school buildings which will facilitate the development of arts studies.

There will be places where rationalisation is not possible and, in such cases, small schools will have to provide second-level education for all the students in a particular area. Education boards will play a key role in ensuring that adequate educational opportunities are available for students in these schools.

Structures for Rationalisation

As in the case of primary schools, the approach to rationalisation will involve co-ordinated action at both national and regional levels. The same approach, including setting up the **commission on school accommodation needs**, will apply at both primary and second level (see Chapter 2).

Young People at Risk

The Department of Education has overall responsibility for the delivery of residential accommodation for children and young persons appearing before the Courts charged with an offence, or on whom custodial sentences have been imposed by the Courts.

There are five custodial centres operating under the Department of Education at present and these centres deliver programmes of care and education. The primary objective of these programmes is the rehabilitation of children who have committed an offence.

The Government recently announced its intention to expand provision in this area to improve the service and to respond to the needs of the Courts. The process of planning these additional facilities is currently under way.

Unfortunately, some of the children and young persons coming into conflict with the law and referred to the custodial facilities have serious emotional and psychiatric problems. It is essential that the system be capable of adequately addressing these needs, where necessary in a custodial environment.

It is also necessary to address the needs of those children who have not committed an offence but for whom placement in a controlled environment is necessary to secure their safety and welfare. The Government has recently announced that arrangements for specialist facilities with a high staff/child ratio will be provided through the health boards to cater for exceptionally disturbed children in need of special treatment, attention and education.

Close co-operation and liaison between the Departments of Education, Health and Justice is particularly important in relation to special care provisions for children and young people. The Government has appointed a Minister of State with special responsibility for child-care provisions in the three concerned Departments. The Minister chairs an inter-departmental committee which has the remit of ensuring the most effective co-operation and liaison between the Departments.

The Minister of State is also responsible for bringing forward the Children Bill, at present being drafted in the Department of Justice. This Bill will comprehensively up-date the legislative framework for dealing with children in conflict with the law.

Framework for Funding

Expenditure

Total expenditure at second level increased from £9.7 million in 1965 to an estimated £861.1 million in 1995. Current expenditure per student at second level has increased nearly threefold in real terms from 1965 to 1994.

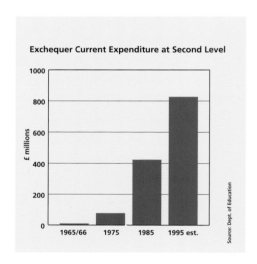

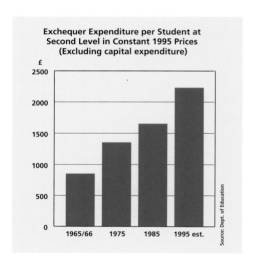

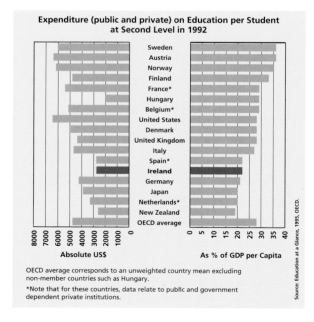

As at primary level, a high proportion of the second-level education budget is non-discretionary. Pay and pensions, mainly of teachers, represent 82 per cent (some £679.8 million) of the current estimated expenditure on second-level education. Existing commitments include pay rates determined centrally through national negotiations.

The number of teachers in the second-level system increased from 6,593 in 1965 to 20,349 in 1993/94, while the number of students increased from 132,000 to 367,645 during the same period, largely on account of the increase in the participation rates at second level.

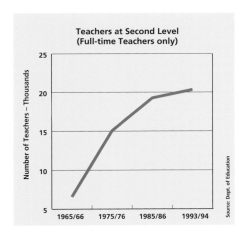

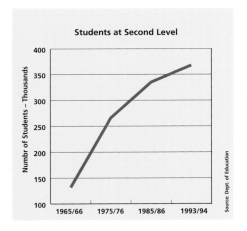

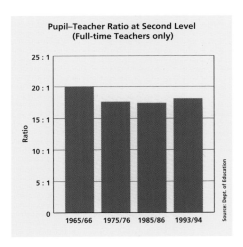

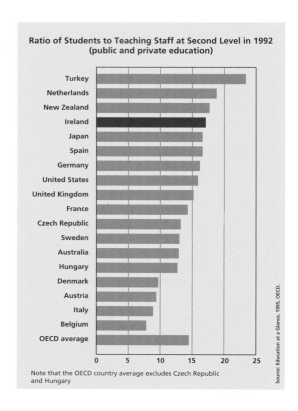

Ratio of Students to Teaching Staff at Second Level in 1992 (public and private education)

Source: Education at a Glance, 1995, OECD.

Note that the OECD country average excludes Czech Republic and Hungary

The balance of £145.8 million in the current estimates for second-level education relates to the non-pay, non-capital requirements of the education system.

Investment in Second-Level Education

The Government is committed to achieving a 90 per cent completion rate at senior cycle by the year 2000. Second-level education is the right of all students who wish to avail of it. Building on the foundation at primary level, second-level education is no longer discretionary for any student and is of central importance in ensuring the student's full participation in economic and social life. Therefore, expenditure on second-level education, in order to meet the projected increase in participation rates – with the consequent diversification of the range of abilities and to prepare students more fully for life, work and further education – is a necessary investment in social and economic well-being.

4 *Further Education*

Vocational Education and Training

Introduction

As well as the courses provided in third-level institutions, a wide range of vocational education and training courses are offered within the education sector for students who have completed second level. The principal programmes are Post-Leaving-Certificate courses. In addition, off-the-job training for apprentices is provided in the Regional Technical Colleges, at the Dublin Institute of Technology and in FÁS Training Centres.

Provision for vocational education and training has grown rapidly since the mid-1980s. However, much of this development, particularly in relation to Post-Leaving-Certificate courses, has taken place in an *ad hoc* and unstructured manner. Accordingly, there is a need to ensure that the future development of vocational education and training, most of which is under the aegis of the Department of Education, takes place in a more cohesive and systematic manner and in a way which is responsive to the needs of students and society.

The Department of Enterprise and Employment and FÁS are also involved in important ways in vocational education and training. There is a need for a more cohesive approach to the development of all vocational education and training to maximise the benefit to students, society and the economy. Accordingly, an important part of the future framework for development will be a more integrated approach by the education and training agencies, involving close liaison between the various agencies and more clearly defined roles and responsibilities. This will take place in the context of the new organisational arrangements set out in this White Paper, including the establishment of the Further Education Authority and the clarification of the respective roles and responsibilities of the Department of Education and the Department of Enterprise and Employment.

Existing Programmes

Post-Leaving-Certificate Courses

Post-Leaving-Certificate courses are principally aimed at those who have completed senior cycle education. Their objective is to provide skills to meet the needs of the economy, to equip young people with the vocational and technological skills necessary for employment and progression to further education and training, and to foster innovation and adaptability in participants. Based on a strong foundation of general education, Post-Leaving-Certificate courses, of one and two years' duration, will continue to be provided. These will focus on:

● technical knowledge – the development of the vocational skills needed for a particular discipline

● personal development – the fostering of interpersonal skills, computer familiarisation and mathematical and literacy skills together with adaptability, initiative and a positive attitude to learning

● work experience – providing the student with work experience, including structured on-the-job training, where feasible, which gives relevance to the skills she/he has learned and an appreciation of an adult's role in working life.

The number of students on Post-Leaving-Certificate courses has increased steadily from approximately 12,000 in 1989 to almost 18,000 in 1995.

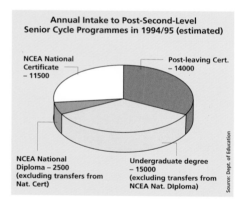

Annual Intake to Post-Second-Level Senior Cycle Programmes in 1994/95 (estimated)

NCEA National Certificate – 11500

Post-leaving Cert. – 14000

NCEA National Diploma – 2500 (excluding transfers from Nat. Cert)

Undergraduate degree – 15000 (excluding transfers from NCEA Nat. Diploma)

Source: Dept. of Education

Apprenticeship

Apprenticeship operates primarily in a number of designated trades, for example, engineering, construction, motor, electrical, printing and furniture. The Government is committed to extending the list of designated trades on a phased basis. This will be the subject of review with the social partners. While traditionally a young person was apprenticed on completion of compulsory schooling, in practice an increasing percentage of apprentices have now already achieved Leaving Certificate standard.

Standards to be achieved in each trade will be measured through on-the-job competence testing, together with modular assessment and formal examinations for off-the-job element. These standards will be agreed between the education sector, FÁS, employers and trade unions. The system for the design and implementation of assessment tests and examinations for off-the-job components will be monitored nationally.

The new system was introduced in September 1993 for fifteen trades with an annual intake of around 500 apprentices. It was extended to a further five designated trades in September 1994 and will encompass the remaining designated trades from September 1995. The target total annual intake into the twenty-four existing statutory designated trades is 3,500.

Rationale for Future Development

The achievement of economic growth and development is dependent significantly on the availability of suitably qualified and adaptable personnel with the necessary personal and vocational skills. The availability of skilled personnel, in turn, is dependent on the efficiency and effectiveness of initial vocational education and training and the updating of skills on a continuous basis throughout life.

The OECD, in its report ***Education and Economy in a Changing Society***, 1989, emphasised that a high standard of general education was an essential prerequisite for a vocationally skilled and adaptable workforce. The report further emphasised the importance for OECD` countries of the role played by initial education and training, before the student entered employment, in promoting successful economic performance and, in broader terms, the functioning of these countries as democratic societies.

Initial and recurrent education and training programmes have a vital role in the enhancement of economic performance. This has been confirmed by studies including the National Economic and Social Council reports ***Education and Training Policies for Economic and Social Development***, 1993, and ***A Strategy for Competitiveness, Growth and Employment***, 1993, the European Union's ***White Paper on Growth, Competitiveness and Employment*** 1994, and the ***OECD Jobs Study – Facts, Analysis, Strategies***, 1994.

The ***OECD Jobs Study*** concluded that "*extending and upgrading workers' skills and competences must be a life-long process if OECD economies are to foster the creation of high-skill, high-wage jobs. Education and training policies should be directed at furthering this goal, as well as at achieving other fundamental social and cultural objectives*" (p. 47). The report emphasised that this would require a major shift in policy in some countries and, in others, the sustained development of existing policies, particularly in relation to the quality of initial education, the transition from formal education to work and the investment in work-related and personal development skills, especially for the least-qualified workers.

An important element of the Government's industrial strategy, arising from the implementation of the ***Report of the Industrial Policy Review Group***, the Culliton Report, 1992, is the priority attached to the acquisition of high quality technical and vocational education.

The rapidly changing social and economic environment requires a high level of flexibility in the labour force and makes it important that all young people receive a general education through which they can acquire broadly based, transferable skills. Current developments in vocational education and training in Europe reflect an increasing emphasis on the provision of a broad occupational training. Such training highlights theoretical understanding, as well as practical skills. This provides the basis for further training, as skill requirements change and become more complex. This approach enables skilled workers both to meet current needs and to be capable of adapting to labour market conditions and future requirements.

The Irish system of general education is well structured to facilitate further development along these lines. The approach to the new senior cycle, as described in Chapter 3, entails expanding the range of vocational options, within an integrated comprehensive second-level system, rather than dividing the senior cycle into parallel general and vocational streams of education. This results in the single-umbrella Leaving Certificate programme, providing a wider range of options for students (see Chapter 3 on Second-Level Education). The further development of vocational education and training will build upon this foundation.

Approach to Policy

The future development of vocational education and training will be based on a number of principles:

- maintaining and enhancing standards of general education as a basis for the development of higher level skills and competencies

- promoting the achievement of high skill levels, coupled with the development of an ethos of innovation and adaptability

- providing comprehensive capabilities; for instance, skills in communication, planning, control and research, integrated with occupational skills and knowledge

- ensuring appropriate equivalence of treatment for different modes of delivery

- providing due recognition for skills, knowledge or competencies received through the different modes of delivery

- improving the co-operation between providers (schools, institutions and teachers) and employers in the identification of the present and future skills and competencies that are required for economic growth and development

- promoting life-long learning, continuous retraining and the updating of skills

- ensuring equality of opportunity for all, through access to quality education and training, on a continuing basis.

Adult and Continuing Education and Training

Context

Learning is a lifelong process, building on the foundation of formal schooling. Access to lifelong education and training is important for all people, and including those who, for whatever reason, completed their formal education without reaching their full potential. Adult and continuing education empowers adults to take a more active and effective part in society.

Adult education and training will be an integral part of the framework for the future development of education. The objective will be to maximise access to suitable programmes for adults who wish or need to update their occupational skills and to continue their personal development, irrespective of their educational and training attainments.

The **Report on the National Education Convention** recorded that "*One of the central problems in Adult Education, until now, has been the lack of a coherent policy. It is clear that a policy framework for adult education is essential. Adult, Community and Continuing Education will be further disadvantaged unless it is brought into the mainstream*" (p. 104). The **Report** goes on to record that the question of structures for the provision of adult education also needs to be examined as a matter of some urgency.

Existing Activities

Provision, at present, includes general adult and continuing education and training and second-chance education, including the Vocational Training Opportunities Scheme and the Adult Literacy Community Education Scheme, in addition to those involving the Area Based Partnerships. Adult Education is characterised by the voluntary nature of participation and the variety of opportunities available from a wide range of sources.

Some postgraduate activities at third level, including management degree programmes and distance education programmes, can also be included in this category.

Vocational Training Opportunities Scheme

The Vocational Training Opportunities Scheme, administered by the Department of Education in conjunction with the Department of Social Welfare, offers the long-term unemployed over the age of twenty-one an opportunity to return to full-time vocational education and training.

The success and achievements of the Vocational Training Opportunities Scheme are widely recognised. The Economic and Social Research Institute, in its evaluation of the community support framework from 1989-1993, describes the Vocational Training Opportunities Scheme as "*a high-quality programme which attempts to provide a bridge back into the education and training system for the long-term unemployed*". The National Economic and Social Council's report, **Education and Training Policies for Economic and Social Development,** 1993, confirmed this evaluation.

Vocational Training Opportunities Scheme courses focus on the development of employment-related skills, including technological and business skills. Modules are also provided on personal development.

Literacy Programmes

Literacy education for adults in Ireland until now has focused on those whose basic literacy skills were inadequate in their day-to-day lives. The Adult Literacy and Community Education Scheme, which is operated through the Vocational Education Committees, provides literacy and basic education tuition on a one-to-one or small-group basis, free of charge or at a nominal cost, with a substantial contribution from volunteer tutors. In addition, literacy tuition is provided by many community and comprehensive schools. Literacy tuition is also provided as part of other programmes such as the Vocational Training Opportunities Scheme and Youthreach and by other agencies such as FÁS and the Irish Congress of Trade Unions, through its Centres for the Unemployed.

In recent years, there has been a trend away from home tuition to centre-based tuition, to the development of student groups and to support from community groups. In general, these provisions have succeeded in meeting demand in that all those coming forward could be accommodated. The success of the programme has tended to attract increasing numbers of adults with literacy difficulties, and resources will continue to be made available to meet their needs.

Basic levels of literacy and numeracy are an indispensable prerequisite for independent living, for access to education and training and for the effective participation in society. Accordingly, **the policy priority will be to ensure**

that suitable and effective programmes are in place for all who wish to overcome literacy and numeracy problems.

Other Programmes

A range of other continuing education and training programmes such as hobby programmes, skill introduction programmes and parenting programmes are provided in a number of second-level schools, in addition to being available to adults through distance learning programmes. These programmes are available to adults, regardless of their educational background or qualifications. A range of programmes is also provided through a number of agencies, for example, FAS.

A policy objective is that learners of all ages will have the opportunity to upgrade knowledge and skills throughout their lives. While some of this new learning will be available in conventional educational institutions, it should increasingly also be available in the workplace and at home, in addition to through professional organisations and community groups.

Approach to Policy

The future approach to adult education policy will involve a number of important considerations:

- the recognition of the central importance of adult education for personal development, for updating knowledge and skills, and for overcoming disadvantage suffered during initial education

- the promotion of life-long learning and continuous retraining and updating of skills

- the integration by schools and colleges of adult education into their mainstream planning processes and the affording of a status to adult education commensurate with its importance

- improving the co-operation between providers (schools, institutions and teachers), and employers in the identification of the present and future skills and competencies that are required for economic growth and development

- the facilitation and encouragement of access by adults to mainstream second-level and third-level education and to vocational education and training, to the greatest extent possible

- the facilitation of course structures which promote adult participation, including modular courses and distance learning

- the continuation of particular provision for adults with special needs, including the long-term un-employed and those with literacy and numeracy problems

- a more integrated approach by the education and training agencies, involving close liaison between the various agencies and more clearly defined roles and responsibilities

- the promotion of close interaction between adult education and more broadly based community development initiatives, for instance, through the Area-Based Partnerships.

Organisational Development

Introduction

The need for an organisational framework arises from the fact that much of the development of provision for both pre-employment vocational education and training and adult education has not taken place in a national context. As the **Report on the National Education Convention** pointed out in regard to adult education *"It is a strength in that it has allowed a rich and varied provision, which attempts to fulfil the needs of a broad range of people . . . its weakness is that there is little long-term planning, no coherent policy for development, duplication of scarce resources, and constant tension and frustration as groups seek access to these limited resources"* (p. 101).

The various elements of vocational education and training will be brought together into a more cohesive and graduated system. This will include employer and trade union interests and will provide the opportunity for all participants to progressively develop their vocational skills and enhance personal development. Equally, more effective adult education for the future will require a more coherent policy framework at national and regional levels, improved organisational arrangements and in-career development for those involved in the design and provision of programmes.

The essential feature of this system will be a co-ordinated set of national arrangements for the provision of vocational education and training, and adult education programmes, and for the national certification of the levels of knowledge and skills attained, as appropriate.

A number of important considerations will underpin the future organisational development of vocational education and training, and adult and continuing education:

- the establishment, at national level, of a framework to co-ordinate development, to advise on and oversee the implementation of policy and to evaluate outcomes

- the assignment of responsibility to the education boards, at regional level, for the implementation of policy and the co-ordination of local delivery arrangements

- the establishment, at national level, of a comprehensive system of certification and validation of awards

- clarification of the respective roles and responsibilities of the Department of Education and the Department of Enterprise and Employment.

The following sections of this chapter deal with co-ordination and certification frameworks at national level, through the establishment of, respectively, a Further Education Authority and of TEASTAS – the Irish National Certification Authority. The roles and responsibilities of the Department of Education and the Department of Enterprise and Employment are also set out in broad terms. The role of the education boards, in relation to regional co-ordination and implementation, is set out in Chapter 14.

Further Education Authority

A Further Education Authority will be established to provide a coherent national developmental framework, appropriate to the importance of vocational education and training (outside the third-level sector) and adult and continuing education. The principal functions of the new Authority will be:

- to advise the Minister in relation to general policy development for the sectors and on particular issues

- the national co-ordination of all vocational education and training, and adult and continuing education

- the allocation of budgets to each education board for (i) vocational education and training and (ii) adult and continuing education provision.

- to ensure a balance of level, type, and variety of programmes to meet student and community needs, including the appropriate location of courses

- to liaise with TEASTAS – the Irish National Certification Authority which will be responsible for validation of standards, the certification of education levels and the establishment of ladders of progression

- to co-ordinate course provision where parallel provision by other Departments or their associated agencies exists, thereby avoiding duplication and overlap, particularly in relation to apprenticeship training.

The Further Education Authority will ensure that each education board has arrangements in place for the continuing identification of educational and training needs and for quality assurance, as well as for monitoring the effectiveness of the programmes in meeting identified needs. The Authority also will be responsible for ensuring, through each education board, that learning and teaching methodologies are developed, taking account of progress in the areas of open and distance learning. Special attention will be devoted to the needs of adult learners, in line with best practice, internationally. It will oversee the establishment of links between education and training and the workplace and ensure that satisfactory guidance and counselling are in place and that individual adult and literacy needs are addressed. The Authority will ensure, through the education boards, that systems and processes are in place in individual institutions and in the system as a whole which facilitate necessary public accountability and provide for the evaluation of cost effectiveness.

All institutions providing vocational education and training, and adult and continuing education will operate policies which promote equality of access, participation and benefit for students and for the wider community

At present most vocational education and training and adult education activity takes place in Vocational Education Committee schools and centres and in community and comprehensive schools. One of the policy objectives will be to encourage a wider range of second-level schools to provide programmes and activities in these areas. Voluntary associations will also continue to be supported in the provision of adult and continuing education.

The composition of the Authority will include representatives of the providers of further education, the social partners, voluntary agencies, the education boards and the Department of Education and the Department of Enterprise and Employment. The Authority will be appointed by the Minister for Education and will discharge its functions within the policy framework set down by the Minister. The Authority will carry out its work through a small expert secretariat.

TEASTAS – The Irish National Certification Authority

Context

The need for a more coherent and effective system of certification for the non-university sector of higher education as well for the vocational training sector is now generally accepted. The **Report on the National Education Convention** recorded widespread approval for such a unified national awards framework. The establishment of such a body is also among the decisions of Government on the report of the Industrial Policy Review Group. In addition, the National Economic and Social Council's report, **Education and Training Policies for Economic and Social Development**, 1993, welcomes the proposal to establish a national education and training certification body. The establishment of this body has been fully endorsed and supported by the European Union, as part of the Operational Programme for Human Resources.

Apart from the universities and the Dublin Institute of Technology, the major course validation and certification authorities in the State are the National Council for Educational Awards and the National Council for Vocational Awards, both operating under the aegis of the Department of Education. Between them, these Councils confer up to 20,000 education and training awards annually. Validation and certification are also carried, for example, by CERT, FÁS, Teagasc and the Farm Apprenticeship Board.

Establishment of a National Certification Authority

The Government has approved the establishment of TEASTAS – the Irish National Certification Authority, under the aegis of the Department of Education. The Authority will have a wide-ranging remit and will be:

- responsible for the development, implementation, regulation and supervision of the certification of all non-university third-level programmes, and all further and continuation, education and training programmes

- responsible for the plans, programmes and budgets necessary for the achievement of the functions set out above, including the plans, programmes and budgets of the National Council for Educational Awards and the National Council for Vocational Awards, which will be reconstituted as sub-boards of TEASTAS

- responsible for the establishment, direction, supervision and regulation of a national qualifications framework

- the national authority/agency for ensuring international recognition for all the qualifications under its remit.

Pending the enactment of the necessary legislation an interim authority will be established on an *ad hoc* basis. Arrangements to give effect to this will be agreed by the Minister for Education (in consultation with the Minister for Enterprise and Employment) with the Minister for Finance.

TEASTAS will have a fourteen-member board, which will bring together all of the business, agricultural, training, and education interests concerned including the social partners.

TEASTAS will provide a structure for the formal involvement of business and the social partners and it will ensure that the needs of business and industry for skilled personnel are met, in particular through improved links between these sectors and the providers of education and training.

The establishment of TEASTAS will facilitate access and progression by individuals through a structured system of graded educational/training qualifications, allowing progression from basic attainments and qualifications up to advanced degree level, in accordance with needs and abilities. This will enhance equality in educational opportunities.

Clarification of the Respective Roles and Responsibilities of the Department of Education and the Department of Enterprise and Employment

It is important to clarify the respective roles of the two Departments in relation to education and training in order to ensure a co-ordinated and focused approach at Government level. Given the importance of education and training and the level of resources involved, it is essential that unnecessary overlap and duplication in provision is avoided and that policy making is co-ordinated on the basis of well-defined roles. This will ensure the more effective use of available resources, thereby maximising benefit to students, society and the economy. Respective roles and responsibilities will be established in accordance with the following broad principles:

- primary policy responsibility in relation to the identification and provision of job-specific and employment-related skills training will rest with the Department of Enterprise and Employment

- primary policy responsibility in relation to all other education and training activities, particularly initial education and training, will rest with the Department of Education; specifically, consultation will take place with the Department of Enterprise and Employment to clarify the role of the Further Education Authority in relation to apprenticeship.

The detailed operational implications of these principles will be worked out between the two Departments. These will include the most effective use of the existing facilities of the education sector and FÁS in relation to the provision of programmes.

The Minister for Enterprise and Employment will publish, at an early date, a comprehensive White Paper on training. This White Paper, and the major public debate which will follow, will provide a valuable contribution to discussions on the clarification of the respective roles and responsibilities of the Department of Education and the Department of Enterprise and Employment.

CHAPTER

5 *Higher Education*

Framework for Development

Context

Higher education promotes social well-being through preserving, widening and advancing the intellectual, cultural and artistic accomplishments of society; through rigorous, sustained and critical evaluations of the past, the present and the possible futures of society; through commitment to the highest standards of research in the various branches of learning; and through equipping society with the particular skills and qualities necessary for economic growth and prosperity.

Society has a responsibility to safeguard the traditional aims of higher education, including the full development of the individual, independent inquiry and the pursuit of knowledge. Higher education institutions in turn have a responsibility to respond to the changing needs of society and the legitimate interests of the State.

The education of students is fundamental to the role of the higher education sector. This teaching function seeks to impart a body of advanced knowledge and to develop the creative, critical, problem-solving and communicative skills of students.

Higher education institutions also have a responsibility, through research, to develop new ideas, new knowledge and new applications of existing knowledge. The availability of new ideas, based on rigorous analysis, is most important for individual development and for economic and social renewal.

Given the multiple purposes of higher education, no single type of institution could carry out effectively all the tasks the system as a whole needs to accomplish. This implies a diversity of institutions with distinctive aims and objectives within a shared philosophy of education. The State will respect the autonomy of the institutions to determine the ways and means through which they will fulfil their particular roles, within the overall aims for the system and the policy framework articulated by the Minister.

Approach to Policy

There are a number of major challenges for institutions and for the State in relation to the future development of higher education:

- the projected growth of numbers participating in higher education

- the increasing diversity in the composition of the student body

- the need to maintain the highest standards of teaching and research

- the need for effectiveness and efficiency at all levels and the growing social and economic expectations of higher education

- the competing needs of other educational and social sectors for resources

- the growing public demand for more accountability in publicly funded institutions.

These challenges influence all levels of the system and raise complex, linked and sometimes competing considerations. **The policy approach will seek to balance institutional autonomy with the needs of public policy and accountability, having due regard to the respective rights and responsibilities of the institutions and the State**. A number of important considerations will underpin this approach:

- the promotion of equality in and through higher education

- the recognition of the legitimate autonomy of institutions, particularly in relation to determining the educational aims and content of programmes

- the promotion of the highest standards of quality

- the preservation of diversity and balance of provision, within the system, while avoiding unnecessary overlap or duplication

- the development of flexible strategies to meet the expanding and changing demand for higher education

- the promotion and facilitation of the key leadership role of higher education as a source of social and economic development, together with the need to ensure continuing relevance to the needs of the economy and the promotion of links between institutions and their social and economic environments

- the continuous development of a framework of accountability for individual institutions and for the higher education system as a whole

- the provision of an appropriate legislative framework, which affirms well-established values while reflecting the role of higher education in modern society.

Development of the Higher Education System

Numbers in third-level education grew from 18,500 in 1965 to almost 91,000 in 1994. These rapidly increasing numbers reflect increasing retention rates at second level, demographic trends and increasing transfer rates into third-level education. In 1980, 20 per cent of the age cohort advanced to third level. This has now increased to over 40 per cent, about half of whom take degree level programmes.

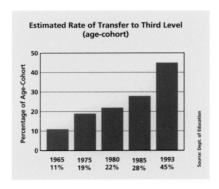

Note: The rate of transfer is estimated by taking total annual intake to all third-level colleges as a percentage of the estimated population at age seventeen. Some persons entering third level may have previously entered. Mature students and entrants from outside the State are also included.

Despite this remarkable growth, the participation rate in third-level education in Ireland lags behind that in most other European countries.

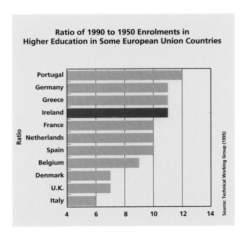

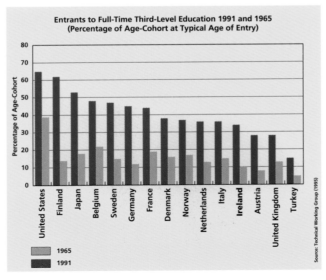

This growth in numbers has been accompanied by a significant increase in the range and diversity of courses and programmes in all institutions. The past twenty years have seen a major transformation in the structure of the third-level sector. This includes the development and expansion of the Regional Technical Colleges, the Dublin Institute of Technology and the two National Institutes for Higher Education. In 1989, the National Institutes were designated as universities and, in 1993, the Regional Technical Colleges and the Dublin Institute of Technology were placed on a statutory footing. During the same period, considerable growth occurred in the university sector, particularly in the disciplines of technology and business. This growth was accompanied by a wide range of innovative developments in the arts and the social sciences.

At the same time, public expenditure (capital and current) on higher education has increased substantially, both in absolute terms and as a proportion of the total budget for education.

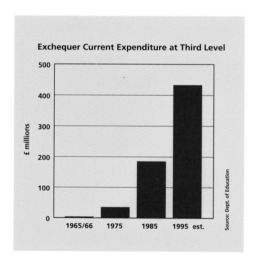

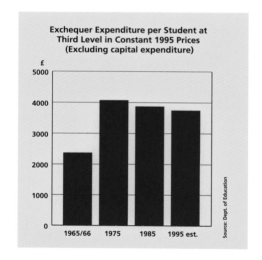

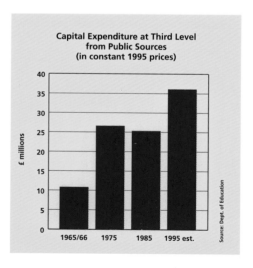

Meeting the demand for higher education places, even with modest growth levels, poses a major challenge for institutions and the State, given the level of resources already devoted to higher education and the strongly competing needs of other sectors.

The ***Interim Report of the Technical Working Group of the Steering Committee on the Future Development of Higher Education*** found that public expenditure per full-time student was above that in a number of European Union countries.

The ***Interim Report*** concluded that, in relation to economic conditions in the country, higher education was well funded when compared with other countries. The report also noted that expenditure on higher education as a percentage of total expenditure on education is close to the OECD average.

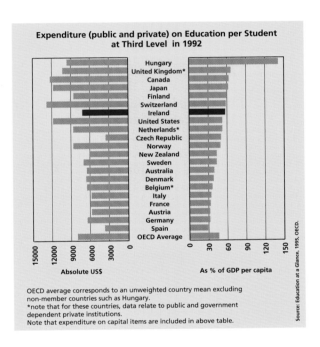

Expenditure (public and private) on Education per Student at Third Level in 1992

OECD average corresponds to an unweighted country mean excluding non-member countries such as Hungary.
*note that for these countries, data relate to public and government dependent private institutions.
Note that expenditure on capital items are included in above table.

Source: Education at a Glance, 1995, OECD.

Structural Issues

Meeting Higher Education Needs

The ***Report on the National Education Convention*** pointed out that

"the extent of additional provision to be made represents an important policy decision. The present strategy of making statistical projections on the likely future demand for places is not a sufficient basis for higher education planning. The setting of enrolment targets for higher education should be made on the basis of an explicit statement of policy objectives and should be accompanied by the appropriate implementation decisions" (p. 91).

The Minister for Education has initiated a major review, in order to develop a policy to meet future higher education needs. A Steering Committee has been established, under the chairperson of the Higher Education Authority, to examine the issues and make recommendations. An *Interim Report* of the Steering Committee's Technical Working Group was published in January 1995.

The Government recognises the importance of third-level education, both for the personal development of students and for social and economic development. It equally recognises the major budgetary implications of continual expansion at third level, in the context of competing demands from other sectors of education, and from public services generally.

As part of the National Development Plan, for the period 1994 to 1999, a substantial programme of capital development is under way amounting to £120 million at 1994 prices. This builds on a similar programme implemented during the period 1989 to 1993. In addition, a number of institutions have shown considerable initiative in securing private funding for development initiatives. The Government will continue to actively support such initiatives.

An important element in formulating future policy options will be the consideration of appropriate targets regarding progression to third-level programmes, to vocational education and training programmes and to employment. Considerations, in this regard, also need to be set in the context of the development of more flexible course structures and progression arrangements in further and higher education. The current operation of colleges, including length of courses and of the academic year, and the optimum utilisation of facilities are also relevant considerations. In view of tight budgetary constraints, measures to maximise the use of facilities and combined public and private funding of capital projects will be important.

The final report of the Steering Committee will be a major input into the formulation of future policy to meet the demand for higher education. The implications of the findings will be considered by the Higher Education Authority. Following receipt of the Authority's advice and recommendations, the Minister will set out policy decisions to meet future demand, having regard to available resources.

System Differentiation

Developments in higher education in Ireland, particularly over the past twenty years, have been based on a differentiated system of third-level education. One part is formed by the universities and the designated institutions under the Higher Education Authority, with state funding allocated by the Authority. The other part includes the Regional Technical Colleges and the Dublin Institute of Technology, with state funding allocated directly by the Department of Education. Both sectors have different and challenging missions. The universities are essentially concerned with undergraduate and postgraduate degree programmes, together with basic and applied research. The main work of the Regional Technical Colleges is in certificate and diploma programmes, with a smaller number of degree programmes and a growing involvement in regionally orientated applied research. However, within each sector and between the two sectors, a diversity of institutions offer differing types and levels of courses.

This system differentiation was discussed at the National Education Convention. Representatives of the universities said they were happy with the present system. They indicated a willingness to facilitate collaboration with non-university institutions and acknowledged the present inadequate student transfer arrangements. However, the *Report on the National Education Convention* also recorded strong pressure within the Regional Technical Colleges sector to resist any centrally determined limit in the range of courses which they offer, because of the benefits for a particular college of having some degree-level work. The *Report* concluded: *"It is unlikely that the resolution of this tension will admit of any single panacea. Optimum decisions will be taken in the light of local circumstances and in the context of national labour market needs. However, in the Analysis of Issues group which discussed this question, it was agreed that if too great an emphasis was placed on degree work, the certificate/diploma work of the RTCs might suffer, and the colleges would fail in their mission to provide the level of skills which they were set up to provide"* (p. 93).

The diversity of institutions and the separate missions of the two broad sectors will be maintained to ensure maximum flexibility and responsiveness to the needs of students and to the wide variety of social and economic requirements.

Role of the Higher Education Authority

The overall co-ordination of the higher education sector, and policy implementation for the sector as a whole, can be determined more effectively if there is a single co-ordinating and funding body for all institutions. The *Report on the National Education Convention* recorded unanimous approval for bringing the Regional Technical Colleges and the Dublin Institute of Technology under the aegis of the Higher Education Authority.

The remit of the Higher Education Authority will be extended on a phased basis to all publicly funded third-level colleges. This development will follow the completion of the current development phase for the Regional Technical Colleges and the Dublin Institute of Technology, including the implementation of new financial and administrative systems, and the legislative reconstitution of the Higher Education Authority. Structured arrangements will be put in place within the reconstituted Authority, which will recognise the distinctive character of the universities and the technological colleges.

The responsibilities of the new Authority will include:

● advising the Minister in relation to higher education policy generally across the whole sector, and on specific issues

- overall responsibility for the operational decisions arising from the implementation of agreed policies, including budgetary allocations to the colleges

- ensuring that all higher education institutions put into effect policies which promote equality of access, participation and benefit for students and, as appropriate, the wider community

- ensuring, within agreed policy parameters, a balance of level, type and variety of programmes among the various institutions, including an appropriate balance between certificate, diploma, degree and postgraduate work, as well as relevance to the occupational and skill needs of the economy

- ensuring that systems and processes are in place which will facilitate the necessary public accountability and provide for the evaluation of cost-effectiveness, within individual institutions and throughout the system as a whole

- ensuring that quality assurance procedures are in place in all institutions and that these procedures are monitored

- promoting links between institutions, society and the economy.

The composition of the Authority will be broadened to include representatives of the Regional Technical Colleges and the Dublin Institute of Technology, as well as representatives of business. The detailed composition will be set out in the amending legislation. The capacity and expertise of the Authority's secretariat will be strengthened to enable it to undertake its wider tasks.

The formulation of policy will remain the responsibility of the Minister and the Government.

Regional Technical Colleges and the Dublin Institute of Technology

Organisation and Management Systems

Work in progress to establish modern financial, management and administrative structures will be continued and completed in Regional Technical Colleges and the Dublin Institute of Technology. Negotiations with the staff unions on more flexible academic staffing structures will continue.

Furthermore, future policy initiatives for the Regional Technical Colleges and the Dublin Institute of Technology will focus on:

- appropriate clarification of the respective roles of Governing Bodies and executive structures within the colleges

- clarification of the powers of the Minister in a number of respects, including taking account of recent court decisions in this regard

- specification of the accountability of the Director of each institution for ensuring efficiency, effectiveness and value for money

- appropriate changes arising from the extension of the remit of the Higher Education Authority, the establishment of TEASTAS and the establishment of education boards.

Course Provision in Regional Technical Colleges

The primary focus of the Regional Technical Colleges will be to provide non-degree level programmes and a limited level of degree provision. The following broad considerations will inform programme provision in the colleges:

- an appropriate balance between the major fields of study in the colleges – Business Studies, Science, and Engineering

- an applied orientation in all programmes

- limited levels of degree provision, taking account of student, economic and social needs, as well as the academic capability of individual institutions to provide degree level programmes

- an appropriately balanced output of graduates from certificate, diploma and degree programmes, with reference to the occupational and skill needs of the economy.

In relation to this latter consideration, the Minister may publish guidelines from time to time, drawing on the advice of the Higher Education Authority and following consultation with the concerned interests.

The Higher Education Authority, in the context of the annual budgetary allocation exercise, will assess and approve applications for programme development from the colleges, in accordance with these guidelines, and regional and national needs. The Higher Education Authority also will report regularly to the Department on the pattern of course development.

Course Provision in the Dublin Institute of Technology

Particular considerations apply to the Dublin Institute of Technology, given its historical development, size and present academic profile. The work currently under way to create a single unified Institute, including the establishment of appropriate academic and administrative structures, will be continued and completed. Given the existing level of degree provision in the Institute, the guidelines in relation to the balance of provision will allow for more degree provision than in Regional Technical Colleges generally, while still maintaining a substantial level of provision at certificate and diploma level.

More Flexible Course Structures

The Higher Education Authority, in co-operation with the institutions, is promoting the co-ordinated development of a system of modular course structures and related credit transfer arrangements. This work will continue.

Flexibility in course structures has the potential to:

- facilitate access

- enable mature and part-time students to study for qualifications while remaining in full-time employment

- facilitate the better use of resources

- facilitate students' transfer between courses and between the technological colleges and the universities

- facilitate the development of a wider range of subject opportunities within courses, for example, modern European languages in business and scientific courses.

Development of the Irish Language

The University of Limerick Act 1989 includes a provision that the university shall have due regard to the preservation, promotion and use of the Irish language. A similar provision is included in the legislation for the Dublin Institute of Technology and the Regional Technical Colleges.

The Higher Education Authority has a particular remit in relation to the national aims of restoring the Irish language and preserving and developing the national culture. **The Department and the Higher Education Authority will co-operate in seeking to develop Irish in third-level colleges generally. A number of initiatives will be undertaken including:**

- the Higher Education Authority will have a statutory responsibility for the preservation, promotion and use of the Irish language in the higher education sector

- the Authority will ensure that discrete budgets to support the use of Irish are assigned within institutions

- each institution will develop an explicit policy for the promotion, development and use of Irish among staff and students on its campus and report on progress annually to the Higher Education Authority

- support will continue for the provision of third-level courses through the Irish language

- consideration will be given to transferring to the Higher Education Authority responsibility for the administration of existing national scholarship schemes.

Links with the Economy

The knowledge and skills of people, coupled with the quality of research and development, have a critical contribution to make to economic competitiveness, prosperity and social cohesion. Higher education institutions have an important leadership role in providing and continually renewing the skills and knowledge-base which are vital to our future progress.

Interaction between higher education institutions and the economy carries considerable benefits for all those involved. This interaction provides significant opportunities for staff to benefit professionally and for students to profit from the staff's experience. It also allows colleges to use their expertise for the benefit of society and the economy. In addition, it opens up new funding sources for the institutions and promotes mutual understanding between business and higher education.

A strong pattern of co-operation has already been established, in research and development and, to a lesser extent, in management and in technical training and retraining. In this respect, the role of the Regional Technical Colleges and the Dublin Institute of Technology has been recognised in the relevant legislation.

There is potential for expanding research and development and for establishing a pattern of support for recurrent technical and management training, through collaboration with the different sectors of the economy. Institutions will be encouraged to expand their activities through an explicit and positive policy on interaction with the economy. Such a policy would provide for:

● research and development and the diffusion of scientific knowledge and technological and managerial innovations

● opportunities for renewal and life-long learning for professional, managerial and technical staff in all sectors of society and the economy

● the putting in place of arrangements for co-operation with business, building on existing best practice, nationally and internationally.

There will be a particular emphasis on collaboration with the indigenous sector of the economy, to promote the highest levels of technological and managerial capacity and in order to encourage Irish firms to employ scientific and technical personnel.

The Higher Education Authority will be responsible for monitoring the policies of the colleges and for providing appropriate support at national level.

Equality

Socio-Economic Disadvantage

A major policy objective of the Government is to promote equality of access to higher education, irrespective of social class, age or disability, for all who have the capacity to benefit from it.

Over the past twenty years higher education has opened up to a much wider range of students from diverse socio-economic backgrounds. Despite this, however, the poorer socio-economic groups are significantly under-represented in higher education.

During the period 1980-1992, rates of admission to higher education increased from 20 per cent to 36 per cent of the relevant age groups. While increases in the proportion of young people proceeding to third level were recorded in almost all socio-economic groups the increases in participation rates were much greater in the better-off groups. For example, the rate of admission of the higher professional group increased from 67 per cent in 1980 to 89 per cent by 1992. At the other end of the social scale, the rate of admission of the unskilled manual group rose from 3 per cent in 1980 to 13 per cent in 1992.

Significantly, also, the only category showing a decline over the period was the salaried employees group. The financial pressures on families slightly above the financial threshold which qualified for student financial support may be a contributing factor to this.

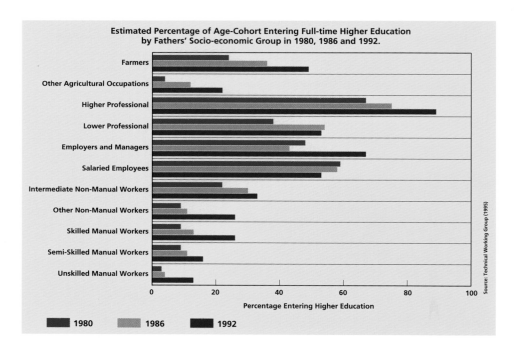

The ***Interim Report of the Technical Working Group of the Steering Committee on the Future Development of Higher Education*** pointed out that *"the social selectivity of higher education as a whole is complemented by further selectivity by sector and field of study . . . students from higher socio-economic groups are significantly more likely to enrol in degree-level courses which tend to lead to better employment prospects and ultimately, higher occupational status. A similar pattern of selectivity is evident with respect to enrolment by field of study, especially within the university sector, where the Higher Professional group is disproportionately concentrated in the professional faculties of Architecture, Medicine and Law"* (p. 122).

The ***Report on the National Education Convention*** concluded that *"while expansion of education provision for the post-compulsory age group does not guarantee greater equality it is an important element in any successful strategy in this area.*

If growth in enrolment is to be accompanied by greater equality, the provision of extra places needs to be supplemented by additional measures targeted at disadvantaged groups, to enable them to avail of higher education" (p. 92).

As with other aspects of education, the promotion of equality of access to participation in and benefit from higher education is a fundamental policy objective. There is no simple or single solution to this problem. Rather, it requires persistent, targeted and regularly evaluated policies which seek over time to redress present imbalances. Educational underachievement is, in many cases, rooted in wider and fundamental social inequalities and differences.

The discussions at the National Education Convention highlighted two main problems with regard to access to higher education. The first was the low proportion of students from lower working-class or disadvantaged backgrounds who sit the Leaving Certificate examination and obtain sufficiently high grades to enter third-level education. The second was the fact that, even when they achieve these grades, a substantially lower proportion enter university than would be expected. This analysis is confirmed in the ***Interim Report of the Technical Working Group of the Steering Committee on the Future Development of Higher Education***. This report also notes that, while the proportion of such students completing in the Leaving Certificate has increased substantially since 1985, significant socio-economic imbalances persist in attainment levels. Significantly, the Technical Working Group also reported that when students secured higher grades in the Leaving Certificate, social or economic class did not significantly influence their chances of proceeding to higher education. However, for students with average or lower attainments in the Leaving Certificate, those from better-off backgrounds were more likely to continue in higher education.

These data confirm that the promotion of equality in education will not be secured by policies focused only on the third-level sector and on the transition from second to third level.

Educational disadvantage has its roots, in many cases, in early childhood. Accordingly, specific initiatives in relation to third-level education are the culmination of the strategies outlined in this White Paper to tackle educational disadvantage throughout a child's schooling. These include initiatives such as pre-school intervention, special support for schools in disadvantaged areas, the restructuring of the senior cycle, providing, where feasible, a comprehensive curriculum for all second-level schools and the removal of selective academic entry tests to schools.

Another important element is the provision of alternative ladders of progression for students through, for example, the certification of vocational education and training programmes, ranging from Youthreach to Post-Leaving-Certificate courses. The long-term objective of these programmes is to minimise educational failure and make it easier for all students to achieve their full educational potential.

Measures at Third Level

In addition to promoting equality at primary and second level there are a number of measures which are taken within the third-level sector to increase participation rates by less well-off students.

Each third-level institution will be encouraged to develop links with designated second-level schools, building upon existing good practice. The purpose of these links will be to support programmes within these schools which promote an awareness and understanding among second-level students and their parents of the opportunities for, and benefits from, third-level education. The short-term objective will be that all designated disadvantaged schools at second level will have formal links with a third-level institution for the purpose of supporting school programmes along those lines. Higher education institutions will be encouraged to hold special "awareness seminars" and open days for students from schools with which special links will be established. These events could be particularly valuable to students during the transition year, on entry to the senior cycle, and on entry to the Leaving Certificate year.

Institutions will be also encouraged to develop appropriate arrangements to help students to make the transition to full-time third-level education. First-year "care programmes", drawing on existing good practice, have an important contribution to make. These could include programmes on study skills, essay writing, project work, library research and examination systems. The range of expertise in third-level colleges offers considerable potential for the development of such high-quality programmes for students. Furthermore, institutions will also be encouraged to make special arrangements for students to be assigned to mentors who can advise and support them on a regular basis during their first year and ease their integration into the college community.

Special training will be provided for staff participating in such programmes. Joint training programmes, involving staff from second-level schools, will also be developed in order to promote mutually supportive approaches.

The Higher Education Authority, in consultation with third-level institutions, will be asked to advise on the most appropriate and effective means of achieving an annual increase in participation of 500 students from lower socio-economic groups in third-level education over the next five years. This objective arises from the recommendation in the *Report on the National Education Convention*.

In the light of the final recommendations from the Steering Committee on the Future Development of Higher Education and the advice of the Higher Education Authority, initiatives will be developed to further facilitate participation by mature students and part-time students, within available resources.

As part of its revised functions, the Higher Education Authority will be responsible for ensuring that each institution develops policies designed to improve access from disadvantaged areas and groups. The effect of these policies will be reported on by the Higher Education Authority.

Student Support Schemes

Although the removal of barriers to more equal participation at third level requires a range of policy measures, fee and maintenance costs are a major constraint. These were mitigated to some extent by the student support schemes. Widespread concern about the equity of the student grant schemes and the regressive impact of income tax relief for covenants led the Government to abolish undergraduate tuition fees in publicly funded third-level institutions. In 1995/96, students will pay half-fees and from 1996/97 on undergraduate fees in these institutions will be abolished. Income tax relief at the standard rate will also be available for fees paid for approved courses in private colleges.

These decisions are a major step forward in the promotion of equality. They remove important financial and psychological barriers to participation at third level. The removal of tax relief on covenants improves tax equity. Tax relief on covenants was regressive. The benefits increased as the level of income increased.

The Student Support Schemes will continue to play an important role in promoting access particularly through the payment of maintenance grants. Significant improvements have already been made. **Further improvements to be implemented following consultation will include the centralisation of the grants application and payments process, the involvement of the Revenue Commissioners in means assessment and the setting up of an independent appeals procedure.**

As further resources become available, priority will be given to increasing the real value of maintenance grants and to reducing and abolishing fees for part-time students.

The criteria for assessing entitlement to grants will continue to be reviewed in order to ensure that the available resources benefit those students who are in greatest need and that public confidence in the system is enhanced.

Special Needs

Special additional arrangements may need to be made to enable people with disabilities to follow third-level courses without difficulty. Third-level institutions will be encouraged to provide special arrangements for students with disabilities. These will build on existing good practice and relevant research. **The Higher Education Authority will pursue a supportive and monitoring role and will actively encourage the development of such special arrangements in all institutions.** The particular arrangements in each institution may include the following:

- consultation with individual students before enrolment to find out what arrangements may be necessary

- individual assessment (as necessary) of entrance and course requirements

- physical access arrangements

- provision of equipment, such as audio equipment for those with impaired hearing, or braille equipment for those with impaired vision

- provision of additional facilities, such as the transcription of taped lectures

- arrangements for counselling

- special examination arrangements, such as time extensions, oral examinations, and technical aids.

The Minister has established a special fund to assist students with physical handicaps. The fund assists individual students and provides services that will benefit various categories of students. Support includes special transport facilities, the provision of special equipment, materials and technological aids and sign language/ interpreters.

The Minister for Education, in collaboration with the Ministers for Health and Equality and Law Reform, has provided funding to Trinity College, Dublin, to undertake a feasibility study on the establishment of a National Institute for Mental Handicap Studies. The feasibility study is reviewing existing provisions for, and needs of, mentally handicapped persons. It will recommend whether an Institute will be established for Mental Handicap Studies and review resource requirements and other implications.

Gender Equality

Full equality between women and men is a fundamental human right. Equally, it is an economic imperative to ensure the full use of the talents of all for the betterment of society. Education has a very important role to play in the creation of a society where all people are treated as equals. All institutions will be asked to develop and publish policies to promote gender equality. These will include:

- policies for the promotion of equal opportunities and associated action programmes, including procedures for preventing the sexual harassment of students and employees

- strategies to encourage increased participation by women students in faculties and courses of study in which they have been traditionally under-represented, including liaison with second-level schools and the preparation and distribution of suitable promotional materials

- appropriate gender balance on all staff selection boards

- encouraging and facilitating women to apply for senior academic and administrative positions.

- the putting in place of arrangements to assist students with young children

The Higher Education Authority will be responsible for monitoring these policies and providing appropriate support at national level. In accordance with Government policy, new education legislation will provide for an appropriate gender balance on all Governing Bodies where it does not apply already. Legislation will build upon the 1994 Regional Technical Colleges and Dublin Institution of Technology Amendment Acts.

Accountability

Quality Assurance

The ***Report on the National Education Convention*** concluded that "*The development of good quality assurance procedures is a central task of management in higher education institutions*" (p. 95). The basis of all educational developments must be to pursue the highest standards of quality for the benefit of students, society and the economy. In higher education, quality is the hallmark which underpins the status and mobility of graduates both nationally and internationally.

The ***Report*** recorded "*total agreement on the need for quality assurance, although it was recognised that its meaning was problematic, and that it might mean different things to different people*" (p. 94). The ***Report***, elaborating on the complexities of the issue, noted:

- that quality assurance brings into sharp relief the conflict between demands for autonomy and accountability

- an acceptance among higher education staff of the need for accountability in the use of public funds

- an anxiety that accountability and efficiency should not extend to relinquishing control of central academic issues.

However, the ***Report*** went on to record that "*this autonomy can only be justified if appropriate and rigorous peer review procedures are put in place. These review procedures should involve assessments of individuals and departments. If third-level institutions are to be self-evaluating, the public interest demands that the mechanisms put in place are manifestly adequate for this purpose*" (p. 94).

The rationale for public accountability derives from the large investment of state funds in educational institutions, the pervasive social and economic impact of third-level education and the extended remit of the Comptroller and Auditor General. Building on the ***Report on the National Education Convention***, public policy in relation to quality assurance in third-level institutions will be guided by a number of considerations:

- recognition of the respective rights and responsibilities of the institutions and the State

- recognition of the primary responsibility of the institutions themselves for putting procedures in place

- an emphasis on rigorous peer review procedures

- a recognition of the need for public accountability in relation to quality and value for money

- the need to ensure that mechanisms in place are adequate for their purpose.

Quality auditing systems will continue to be developed by the institutions under the overall direction of the Higher Education Authority. These will focus on:

- the cyclical evaluation of departments and faculties by national and international peers, preceded by an internal evaluation by the department or faculty

- arrangements for the implementation and monitoring of evaluation findings

- the development of appropriate performance indicators, including national and international comparisons.

These systems will underpin the achievement and maintenance of the highest levels of quality, which is a central aim of both institutions and the State. Systems will be set up to evaluate the effectiveness of research, of teaching and of links with the wider community.

The restructured Higher Education Authority will be responsible for monitoring and evaluating the systems within individual institutions. In close consultation with the institutions, the Authority will develop a framework for reporting on the results of quality evaluations and the effectiveness of procedures, including the development of appropriate performance indicators. This will ensure that relevant information in relation to the outputs of quality evaluations is available to the Higher Education Authority and to the Minister as a basis for policy formulation. Furthermore, the Authority will ensure that information is made available to the general public.

The ***Report on the National Education Convention*** concluded that *"A necessary complement to the process of evaluation of quality is the need for a development programme which will assist third-level staff in improving their teaching skills. Quality teaching is no less an imperative at third level than it is at first and second level"* (p. 94). **The putting in place of a comprehensive programme for the development of teaching skills for third-level staff will be a priority**. Specific provision for this will be made in the allocation for in-career training in the National Development Plan.

Funding

New unit-cost funding arrangements are being developed by the Higher Education Authority, in collaboration with the institutions. These will continue to be developed by the Authority to ensure that available resources, deployed across the sector as a whole and within institutions, are most effectively used for the maximum benefit of students. Within the agreed budgets for the institutions and subject to Government policy in relation to the sector, institutions will be responsible for deploying their resources in a cost-effective and efficient manner.

The Higher Education Authority will be responsible for the co-ordination of the development of financial management and accounting procedures and management information systems for all third-level institutions.

University Legislation

Universities are complex institutions in terms of the range of activities carried out, their internal academic and administrative structures, the increasing diversity of the student body and the very large budgets involved. Accordingly, effective management structures are critically important. The ***Report on the National Education Convention*** concluded that "*third-level institutions are difficult to manage and require constant reappraisal of management structures and functions*" (p. 95).

Arising from the Government decisions on the implementation of the Culliton and Moriarty Reports, there is a commitment to a broadening of the composition of the Governing Bodies of universities in order to provide wider representation from society and the economy. In addition, academic staff, non-academic staff and students will have statutory representation on all Governing Bodies, coupled with appropriate provisions to ensure gender balance on Governing Bodies. There will also be statutory provision for Ministerial nominees on all Governing Bodies. **New legislation in relation to Governing Bodies will be introduced this year.**

The Minister will also proceed this year with the amendment of the National University of Ireland legislation, on the basis of proposals put forward by the Senate of the National University of Ireland. Under these proposals, the existing constituent colleges at Dublin, Cork and Galway, as well as the recognised college at Maynooth, would become constituent universities of the National University of Ireland. The constituent universities would have greater freedom in matters such as staff appointments, establishment of programmes, marking standards and examinations. The National University itself would continue to appoint external examiners and award qualifications.

More comprehensive legislation for the university sector as a whole will also be introduced. This will seek to underpin a number of the principles set out in this chapter:

● regard for proper institutional autonomy, coupled with appropriate public accountability

● affirmation of the ethos and tradition of universities, together with changes, to reflect the role of universities in modern society

● preservation of the diversity of universities

● the enhancement of the developmental role of universities.

Legislation would also set out, in appropriate form, the roles and functions of governing bodies and executive structures, respectively. The role of the university president as accounting officer will also be set out. The Minister will issue a position paper to the universities, following consultation with the Higher Education Authority, outlining further her approach to legislation and the principles underpinning it.

Research

This chapter has already referred to the different missions of universities and technological colleges. Universities are mainly concerned with undergraduate and postgraduate degree level programmes, together with basic and applied research. Technological colleges (with special considerations applying to the Dublin Institute of Technology) focus mainly on certificate and diploma programmes, with a smaller number of degree programmes and a growing involvement in regionally orientated applied research.

The role of universities as discoverers and disseminators of knowledge sets the context within which links emerge between research and teaching. The value of research also reaches into the spheres of technological development and international competitiveness: the higher education sector is a major supplier to research efforts in Ireland. In the ten-year period, 1982 to 1992, expenditure on research in the higher education sector increased in real terms by 200 per cent.

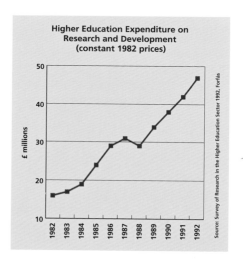

The ***Report on the National Education Convention*** stated that "*there would be a general welcome for the development of a more explicit national policy on the funding of research in third level education*" (p. 97). In relation to the block grant to colleges, the ***Report*** stated that "*the unified budget which forms the block grant to colleges would provide the basic level of research funding. It is accepted that selectivity would arise in relation to additional funding for which academics would be encouraged to bid*" (p. 97).

In moving to a more explicit policy in relation to research, the Department will take into account the consultancy study in relation to university research and its funding, which is being carried out under the aegis of the Higher Education Authority, as well as the relevant recommendations made by the Science Technology and Innovation Advisory Council.

A number of important principles will inform a research policy for the third-level sector:

- the unified teaching and research budget, which forms the block grant to colleges, will be continued; it will provide the basic level of research funding

- the role of research in course development and the advancement of knowledge in all disciplines will be recognised

- any additional funding for research will be provided as a separate budget, for which competitive bidding will be the norm with independent assessment by international peers on research proposals

- within the education sector, most basic and strategic research will be predominantly in the universities while the focus of the technological colleges will be on applied regionally orientated research

- the role of research in technological development and international competitiveness will be recognised

- the need to develop centres of excellence involving co-operation between institutions and disciplines, particularly in expensive research areas, will be examined.

Within this framework, **each institution will develop and publish an explicit policy on its approach to research**, including the broad balance between research and teaching commitments within disciplines. The policy will also set out the key aims of research activity and the principal criteria for evaluating the effectiveness of research within the institutions.

Private Colleges

Regulation of Private Colleges

There has been significant growth in recent years in the number of private commercial colleges.

In future, such institutions running courses which receive State certification for their awards will be subject to new control regulations. Regulation of these colleges is important in order to:

- guarantee the academic integrity and quality of the courses and qualifications on offer

- prescribe institutional norms in regard to, for instance, staff qualifications, support services, teaching/ research balance, entry standards and the balance of course provision

- protect the financial investment of students and their parents.

The primary focus of policy, therefore, will be to ensure the quality of provision in these institutions and to provide for adequate consumer protection.

To date, a number of private commercial colleges have been designated under the National Council for Educational Awards Act 1979. These designations have taken place, within guidelines prepared by the Department, following an evaluation of the institution by the National Council for Educational Awards. Also, some of the designated colleges have chosen to have courses validated by agencies outside the State rather than by the National Council for Educational Awards. At present, there are no arrangements to ensure consistency and rigour in the appraisal and evaluation of quality of these courses.

New control procedures will be put in place in relation to private commercial colleges offering third-level programmes which seek State certification. Implementation of these procedures will be the responsibility of TEASTAS – The Irish National Certification Authority. The procedures will cover the following:

- rigorous evaluation of the quality of courses on offer, not just courses validated by the National Council for Educational Awards

- evaluation of the physical and educational facilities, teaching staff and other support services available in the institution

- an institution will not be given formal National Council for Educational Awards designation in the future, unless it already has at least three courses of certificate or diploma standard

- in future, each institution will require as a condition of National Council for Educational Awards designation that fully satisfactory arrangements are in place to guarantee the recoupment of students' investment in the event of the institution's commercial failure

- all designated institutions will be obliged to make available relevant statistical information to the Department of Education and National Council for Educational Awards.

In addition, arrangements will provide that there is a regular evaluation of the quality and standards in recognised institutions, as a condition for continuing approval.

Approved courses in such designated institutions will be eligible for tax relief on fees from 1996 onwards.

The Minister will publish a code of practice incorporating these principles. Appropriate legislative underpinning for the code will also be provided.

6 *Sport*

Aims

Sport covers a wide range of activities, including organised competitive sport, recreational sport and active leisure pursuits within the *Sport for All* concept. The value of participation in sport and active leisure pursuits in the physical, psychological and social development of the individual is well documented and accepted.

Most adults have become increasingly concerned about issues affecting health and well-being and are more aware than ever of the value and pleasure of physical exercise and sport. However, this is not always accompanied by a readiness to take part in any form of regular exercise. There is a need, therefore, to translate this awareness into regular participation.

Sport is an essential element of the balanced lifestyle which is necessary for healthy living, enjoyment and socialisation. It also has the capacity to promote increased economic activity, not only through the manufacture and supply of equipment, but also as an important and growing service industry within the community and as an asset in attracting foreign tourists. Outstanding performances by Irish sportspersons in the international arena increase morale at home and enhance the country's prestige and image internationally.

The specific aims of sports policy will be to facilitate individuals and groups, as far as possible, to participate in physical recreation and sporting activity and to offer appropriate opportunities for every individual – regardless of sex, age or ability – to continue the practice of sport and physical recreation throughout their lives. This will build upon positive attitudes to physical well-being cultivated in formal schooling. In co-operation with the appropriate sports organisations, a further aim of sports policy will continue to be to ensure that people with interest and ability have the chance to improve their standard of performance in sport.

Policy Approach

Participation in sport and physical recreation will continue to be supported by the Department of Education through the provision of grant-aid for:

- appropriate facilities

- a range of educational, promotional and support programmes designed to increase participation, improve performance and achieve excellence

- support for appropriate training and development programmes for administrators, development officers, instructors, sport leaders, and coaches at all levels.

The education boards will have a key role in the management and co-ordination of the sports policy in their areas.

Sport for All

As a member of the Council of Europe, Ireland is committed to the implementation of the *Sport for All Charter* which was introduced in 1978. This charter seeks to extend the benefits of sport to as many people as possible irrespective of age, sex or ability. A variety of *Sport for All* promotions has been organised, aimed at the less-active population, in co-operation with the Vocational Education Committees and with considerable voluntary support.

The effectiveness of *Sport for All* initiatives in Ireland, to date, has been severely limited by the absence of formal structures at local level to co-ordinate the development and delivery of programmes and to promote the necessary co-ordination and co-operation between voluntary sports and other community and public-sector organisations. In future, **the education boards will have a major role in the development and implementation of sport and physical recreation programmes, in support of local community interests and sports organisations**. Sports Development Officers will be employed by the education boards whose role will be to co-ordinate the efforts of all sports leaders working in the community, encourage participation in sport and physical activity by all age groups, and develop close school-community links and full use of existing resources.

School-Community Links

There is a close relationship between the physical education programme in schools and sports in the community. Sport in the community is generally organised by clubs affiliated to national governing bodies, many of which organise competitions for schools. The traditional involvement of teachers in sports organisations provides the type of dynamic link which can benefit both the school and local sport organisations. These links ensure that the games and recreation activities, that are a part of community life, are integrated, in a suitable form, into the school programme. In this way, the school can also be a factor in enriching community life. By identifying the relationship between school activities and life outside school, young people will have an opportunity of seeing physical education as a part of their lifestyle and not just as a separate school activity.

There has been considerable investment of public funds in sports and recreation facilities, both in schools and for the community. It is important that maximum benefit should accrue from this investment. In this respect, the shared use of sports and recreational facilities between schools and colleges and the wider community offers substantial opportunities for the efficient use of resources, through ensuring that they are in use throughout the year and by avoiding a duplication of provision.

There are corresponding opportunities for the use of community facilities by schools. This is a significant feature of the current sports capital programme, under which many facilities are sited close to schools, with appropriate access for school purposes. The education boards will have an important co-ordinating and management role in this regard.

Sporting Excellence

In recent years, the performances of Irish sportspersons in top level international sport have been significant and have brought credit to themselves and to the country and immense pleasure to many people.

Grants are paid to national governing bodies of individual sports to assist in the administration and the development of their sports, as well as to assist them in participating in international competitions abroad and in hosting major international events at home. This support will continue.

Funding is also made available to individual sportspersons to enable them to train on a full-time basis, with some degree of financial independence. In addition, one objective of the continuing development of capital facilities throughout the country is to provide for the training and competitive needs of sportspersons.

Research and Development

There is a need to continually evaluate the effectiveness of programmes and initiatives in improving performance and increasing participation. Thus, the Department will adopt a proactive approach to the selection of research projects and will continue to support relevant initiatives to:

● measure the outcomes and success of programmes supported by the Department against pre-identified objectives and thereby the more effective use of resources

● provide accurate information on participation rates in, and attitudes towards, sport and physical activity by the general population

● assess the effectiveness of programmes aimed at top-level performers

● identify the need for the provision of facilities for particular sports and locations for the provision of recreational facilities, with particular regard to the needs of disadvantaged areas.

7 Youth Work

Aims

The ***Report of the National Youth Policy Committee***, 1984, defined the main aim of youth work as *"[to] offer young people, on the basis of their voluntary involvement, developmental and educational experience which will equip them to play an active part in a democratic society, as well as meeting their own personal developmental needs"* (p. 114). As well as fulfilling this aim, youth work provides opportunities for young people to recognise and develop their talents and skills in a process of learning by doing and reflecting on the experiences.

Present Position

The Department of Education supports, by way of financial assistance, a range of national voluntary youth organisations which meet educational and other criteria, including voluntary adult involvement and the active participation of young people in the running of their organisations. The national voluntary youth organisations carry out the vast majority of the activities in the youth work area.

In addition, a number of agencies at local level provide support services for all the organisations involved in youth work activities in a particular area which are not affiliated to any larger organisation, such as clubs, projects and community groupings, as well as local units or groups of national organisations. These support services seek to improve the effectiveness of local communities and youth organisations in responding to the needs of young people. The services include training, programme development, information, advice and special initiatives catering for the needs of young people in areas of disadvantage.

Almost half of the annual youth work budget is spent on special projects to assist disadvantaged youth. This fund, from the proceeds of the National Lottery, provides finance to support out-of-school youth work programmes and services for young people in particular need. Grants for specific projects are allocated to organisations and groups, including voluntary organisations, Vocational Education Committees and health boards. These projects seek to address the needs of young people who are disadvantaged due to a combination of factors such as unemployment, social isolation or drug or substance abuse. Approximately 200 projects around the country are now aided in this way.

These initiatives, together with the major contribution made by the national voluntary youth organisations to disadvantaged areas, have highlighted the contribution that youth work can make to the lives of young people in disadvantaged communities. Very often such young people's experience of the formal education and training system is either partly or wholly negative. An important objective of youth work is to facilitate the return of these young people to the formal education or training systems. In addition, youth work can help to counteract the experience of alienation, to restore a sense of self-esteem and to support positive action which will develop potential.

Grants are also provided for youth information services. These services are provided, in various centres throughout the country, through the Vocational Education Committees and voluntary youth organisations.

Development of Policy

In future, policy development will be informed by a recognition of youth work as a planned, systematic educational process which assists and enhances the personal and social development of young people, which is complementary to defined curricula and which is implemented primarily by voluntary groups and organisations.

Some aspects of youth work policy are best addressed at national level and others at regional or local level.

The voluntary nature of youth work provision will be enhanced and developed in the new proposals for the development of youth work. In particular, a number of initiatives will be developed. It is proposed to extend on a nationwide basis, within available resources, the arrangements, now limited to a few areas, under which grant aid may be given to local voluntary groups engaged directly in work with young people.

Revised guidelines for a single model of a Voluntary Youth Council will be developed to provide a forum for local youth groups and units to have an input into the formulation and implementation of youth work policy and provision. Support will also be provided for the provision and accreditation of training for professional and voluntary youth workers.

Overall national policy on youth work will continue to be a responsibility of the Department of Education, in consultation with the voluntary youth organisations and appropriate statutory bodies. The funding of recognised voluntary youth organisations at national level will also continue to be provided by the Department.

The Government recognises that the present diversity of provision, represented by the many specialist and unitary organisations, ensures a broad range of services. However, the needs of young people should be clearly articulated in a co-ordinated manner at national level. This can best be facilitated through a unified voice emanating from a single representative body for all voluntary youth organisations.

The need for specific youth services in any particular region or locality can best be assessed by a regional or local body, having regard to the requirements of the area. There is a need for the further empowerment of local communities to play a role in the development of responses to the needs of young people in youth work. Gaps in provision at local or community level need to be identified, with priority being accorded to the youth work needs of the disadvantaged areas.

It is envisaged, therefore, that each education board, will be given statutory responsibility for the co-ordination and development of youth work as an integral part of its overall responsibilities in the areas of formal and non-formal education. Recognised voluntary youth organisations will continue to play a major role through their involvement in the delivery of services to young people.

The functions of the education boards will include:

- the identification of local youth needs, paying particular attention to the needs of disadvantaged young people

- liaison with voluntary organisations at regional level

- development of links between youth work, adult and community education and formal education, having particular regard to the needs of disadvantaged young people

- development of effective networking at regional level among community, voluntary and statutory interests involved in youth work and between those involved in youth work and other services, such as adult education, sport and recreation, the home-school links scheme, and other social services

- the introduction of a mechanism for the monitoring and evaluation of the effectiveness and efficiency of initiatives funded by the board, in accordance with guidelines issued by the Department

- the allocation of resources provided by the Department of Education in response to the Board's youth work development plan. This plan should be prepared having consulted widely with interested parties in addition to the carrying out of relevant research to establish priorities.

To carry out their youth work functions, a Youth Development Officer will be employed by the education boards. This post could be incorporated with the Sports Officer post and could, in some areas, be filled by way of reassignment.

A National Youth Advisory Committee will be established bringing together the relevant Government Departments and statutory agencies involved in the delivery of services to young people and, through a single representative body, recognised voluntary youth organisations.

The functions of this National Advisory Committee should include advising the Minister on:

- all matters relating to the provision of comprehensive and integrated youth development strategies and services

- youth service policy development and implementation
- the co-ordination, provision and evaluation of services to young people.

Evaluation

There is a need for a fully comprehensive system of evaluation, research and monitoring of all youth work provision, in order to facilitate the transfer of good practice and assess the effectiveness of grant-aided initiatives. A comprehensive system of monitoring and evaluation will be established featuring:

- a requirement for the continuing self-evaluation of all grant-receiving organisations and initiatives
- a monitoring and evaluation capacity within the Department
- a monitoring and evaluation function at regional level by the education boards.

This system will be introduced on a phased basis.

The Department of Education, in consultation with the relevant parties, will draw up criteria for determining the distribution of grant aid, both by the Department and through education boards.

Youth Information

The network of youth information centres will be further developed, particularly in disadvantaged areas. Particular emphasis will be placed on the integration of these centres into local youth services, on their outreach work and their involvement of volunteers from local communities.

Legislation

The ***Government of Renewal*** policy document includes a commitment to *"prepare a Youth Service Act to provide a statutory basis for developing youth work in Ireland"* (Para. 111 p. 31). This Act will set down the statutory responsibility of the Minister for Education and the education boards in relation to youth work.

Part

3

The Teaching Profession

8 *The Teaching Profession*

Context

The quality, morale and status of the teaching profession are of central importance to the continuing development of a first-class education system in the decades ahead. Irish teachers are highly regarded, and the profession continues to attract people of high calibre and commitment. The *Report on the National Education Convention* confirmed the *"high valuation of the professional and caring tradition of the Irish teaching force"* (p. 85).

Teachers have made an enormous contribution to Irish society. The profession's standing has also been recognised internationally. It is important, therefore, that the career of teaching continues to attract talented people and that it proves professionally rewarding to those who follow it. The *Report on the National Education Convention* recorded the concern *"that the status and profile of the teaching profession should be maintained and developed so as to attract applicants of high quality, both male and female"* (p. 85).

The Importance of Teacher Education and Training

The knowledge and skills of the teacher, which include a deep understanding of the subject matter to be taught and of learning and pedagogical theories, critically determine the quality of education in schools. The teacher has the onerous responsibilities of imparting knowledge and equally importantly of organising learning in the classroom, taking account of their students' wider experience at home and in the community.

As with other professions, and because of changing social and economic circumstances, initial teacher education cannot be regarded as the final preparation for a life-time of teaching. The *Report on the National Education Convention* recorded wide support for the view of *"the teaching career as a continuum involving initial teacher education, induction processes and in-career development opportunities, available periodically throughout a teacher's career"* (p. 85).

Expenditure on teachers (pay and pensions), which accounts for over 80 per cent of the total education budget, further underlines the long-term importance of quality pre-service education, well-managed induction procedures, in-career development programmes throughout the teaching career, as well as conditions of service which facilitate flexibility and adaptability, in response to curricular and societal change.

The challenges posed for teacher education, both in-career and pre-service, were examined in the ***Report on the National Education Convention*** which stated, *inter alia*: *"In the context of many new changes in aspects such as subject content, pedagogical style, assessment procedures, relationships with parents and community, changes in the pupil clientele and social conditions, new approaches to in-school planning, new technologies and the more extended role of the school, new approaches and responses are required from initial and inservice teacher education"* (p. 85).

Conditions of service are of central importance to teachers and crucially influence the effectiveness of schools. The major changes in the current reform of education pose significant challenges for the conditions in which teachers work. In this regard, teachers will be given the opportunity to assume a major responsibility for the regulation and monitoring of standards within their profession.

Primary Pre-Service Education

The ***Report on the National Education Convention*** records a strong preference for the retention of the present concurrent model of teacher preparation. In this model, the students concentrate on specific academic subjects and educational theory, while at the same time practising teaching in the classrooms. **The concurrent model of teacher education will be retained for the initial training of primary teachers**. The fundamental aim of courses is to provide the professional and academic foundation for teachers' careers, by providing a third-level education which will impart the knowledge and pedagogical skills necessary to teach the primary school curriculum.

Pre-service courses should not be narrowly confined to the immediate requirements of the system but should include the personal education and development needs of students. In future, they will be complemented by structured induction programmes as well as by properly co-ordinated in-career development provision. The ***Report on the National Education Convention*** maintained that such developments *"could (also) allow for beneficial reorganisation within preservice courses, which, at present, tended to be very full because of the absence of a structured inservice scheme"* (p. 87).

The linkages between colleges of education and universities provide an opportunity for the continual development of pre-service courses, in the light of continuing changes to the primary curriculum. There will be an emphasis, in pre-service courses, on combining academic study with the study of educational theory and practice directed towards the requirements of the primary school curriculum.

In response to the recommendations of the ***Report of the Review Body on the Primary Curriculum*** and the ***Report of the Primary Education Review Body***, pre-service education now lays special emphasis on the development of a broader range of competencies within an integrated curriculum, particularly in the teaching of the arts, European awareness, health promotion, music, physical education and science, and on catering for children with special educational needs.

Primary teachers graduate with both an academic specialisation and a professional qualification. Academic specialisations could be more fully used for the benefit of the teacher and the school, if selected teachers, with appropriate induction, became curriculum leaders in their subject specialisation. Curriculum leaders would work with teachers in their schools or other schools in the region. For this reason, schools will be encouraged to draw upon teachers' specialisations to be curriculum leaders for particular subjects. **Each education board will be responsible for developing schemes to facilitate the curriculum leaders in providing services to a number of schools**.

Mature entrants to colleges of education, who have a variety of backgrounds and experiences, enrich the primary teaching profession. The primary sector and teaching profession benefit from the participation of mature students in pre-service courses. The courses for graduates in other disciplines have also been a welcome development. The present arrangements for these purposes will be further developed, in consultation with the colleges of education. The arrangements will have regard to the projected demand for primary teachers and will include the specification of entry standards and the development of access courses for mature students.

Teachers' competence in the Irish language decisively influences the quality of teaching of Irish in schools and the standards reached. Colleges of education are obliged to ensure that all primary teachers have the oral competence necessary for effective Irish language teaching. **In order to enhance standards in this regard, a more rigorous oral/aural Irish examination will form part of the assessment for all student teachers throughout their education and training**.

There is a need to strengthen and prioritise the education of student teachers in the creative and performing arts and in the scientific aspects of the social and environmental programme, if they are to give effect to the changes sought and outlined in this White Paper. Consideration will be given to the means by which the completion of a full Leaving Certificate course in the creative and performing arts, as well as in a scientific or technological subject, will be encouraged for prospective entrants to colleges of education.

A key responsibility of the colleges of education during the teacher education programmes will be to evaluate students' teaching potential. The objective of such an evaluation will be to identify, at the earliest possible point, students who are unsuited to teaching.

Second-Level Pre-Service Education

The majority of second-level teachers qualify either by taking a primary degree, in one or more academic subjects, followed by a one-year professional course leading to a Higher Diploma in Education, or by taking concurrent training courses in such subjects as home economics and physical education.

While the vast majority of second-level teachers have a teaching qualification, teachers in the Vocational Education Committee sector are not required to have a general teaching qualification. However, in practice, the majority of teachers now entering this sector do have a professional qualification. In future, **it will be a requirement for new entrants to have a general professional teaching qualification in order to teach in any second-level school**.

At present, universities adopt a variety of approaches in their Higher Diploma in Education programmes. There has been no comprehensive evaluation at national level of the effectiveness of the Higher Diploma in Education. Some disquiet has been expressed about the adequacy of the Higher Diploma in preparing students for a career in teaching. The ***Report on the National Education Convention*** while recognising that the Higher Diploma has adapted flexibly to changing needs, stated that *"this process needs to be maintained on a continuous basis and with a clear sense of direction"* (p. 86).

Taking full account of best practice developed in the present models of pre-service education for second-level teachers, including the consecutive and concurrent models, **the Higher Education Authority will be asked to undertake a systematic review of pre-service education for second-level teachers** and to make recommendations for its future development. This review will be carried out in co-operation with the teacher education institutions and the Department of Education, and in consultation with the concerned interests. In carrying out the review, the Higher Education Authority will have regard to the following important features which should underpin the professional preparation of second-level teachers:

- the maintenance of a mutually reinforcing balance between the personal and professional development of students, as well as between the theoretical and practical aspects of their professional preparation

- the development of a firm understanding of the foundation disciplines of modern educational theory and practice which would equip student teachers for successful careers in a changing environment

- the development of an understanding and appreciation of the role of the educational system at all levels and, in particular, the ways in which second-level schools contribute to that role

- the acquisition of the knowledge and skills which will enable student teachers to formulate and examine educational objectives, to develop and implement programmes of study, and to match these with appropriate methodologies and modes of assessment

- the development of a good understanding of adolescent development and behaviour and of the social context of the schooling of adolescents, including an understanding of gender equality

- the provision of an extensive programme to develop the pedagogical and classroom management skills of student teachers through wide and varied teaching practice, including placement in different school settings and teaching subjects at various levels

- the use of experienced teachers to guide and assist student teachers and to facilitate their subsequent induction into teaching.

As in the case of the colleges of education, a key responsibility of the second-level, pre-service education institutions during the teacher education programmes will be to evaluate students' teaching potential. The objective of such an evaluation will be to identify, at the earliest possible point, students who are unsuited to teaching.

Teacher education institutions will ensure that all teachers have a basic qualification in Irish and, for those who will teach Irish or through the medium of Irish, the competence necessary for effective Irish language teaching. The Higher Education Authority, in carrying out its review, will be asked to evaluate present standards and make recommendations for the future.

Development of the Induction Year for Primary and Second-Level Teachers

The quality of a teacher's experience during the early years of teaching is critical to developing and applying the knowledge and skills acquired during that initial training, and also to forming positive attitudes to teaching as a career. **A well-developed and carefully managed induction programme, coinciding with the teacher's probationary year, will be introduced for first- and second-level teachers**. The National Education Convention "*gave a general welcome to the . . . proposal for a structured induction year into teaching, following initial training*" (**Report**, p. 86).

A good induction programme will provide teachers, in their first full year, with the opportunities to apply the knowledge and skills acquired during initial training and to master a broad range of new knowledge and skills, including a deeper understanding of the internal organisation of schools, the curriculum and its application to different ability groups, classroom management skills, and systems of assessment and reporting. The ability to evaluate their own performance and identify their strengths and weaknesses, as well as areas requiring further development, can also be acquired during this year.

It is envisaged that newly appointed teachers will be supported by both teacher education institutions and schools. Teacher education institutions will maintain links with the newly qualified teachers by providing additional opportunities for learning to supplement those already provided in initial training courses, for example, in the form of occasional, short modules. Schools will contribute to the induction process by providing mentors whose task it will be to advise the newly appointed teachers and, together with the school principal, to liaise with the teacher education institutions, on the teacher's further professional development needs. The arrangements for providing mentors will be developed in the context of revised in-school internal management structures (see Chapter 11).

As part of the induction programme, teacher education institutions will prepare profiles of student teachers for the schools. These profiles will include details on training already undertaken, indicate personal strengths and particular expertise, as well as areas requiring further development. These profiles will be updated at the end of the induction period and will form the basis for the preparation of personal development plans for the newly qualified teachers. These plans will be regularly updated throughout the teachers' careers and will form the basis for planning the further professional development of these teachers.

Towards the end of the induction year, school principals, after consultation with mentors and the teacher education institutions, will formally assess and make a recommendation on the suitability of new entrants for registration by the Teaching Council (see section below dealing with a Teaching Council). This certification process will apply to all new teachers at primary and second-level. In order to ensure the highest standards in this critical selection, the Regional Inspectorate will carry out an independent evaluation of the suitability of a representative cross-section of teachers, before their final registration.

The effective implementation of the induction year will require detailed planning. This will be undertaken in consultation with the relevant interests.

In-Career Professional Development of Teachers

Context and Aims

A consistent theme running through the debate on the reform of the education system is a unanimous acceptance of the need for a cohesive national policy on, and a comprehensive programme of, in-career professional development for teachers, related to the long-term development of the teaching profession and the education system generally.

In-career professional development for teachers is part of the continuum which builds upon the foundations laid in pre-service education and induction. The *1991 OECD Review* concluded that the challenges that face the teaching profession in Ireland are *"how to address in a comprehensive way the needs and aspirations of talented and well-educated young teachers . . . as they progress through their careers . . . we believe that the best returns from further investment in teacher education will come from the careful planning and construction of a nationwide induction and in-service system using the concept of the teaching career as the foundation"* (p. 98).

The fundamental aims of in-career professional development programmes are to equip teachers with the capacity to respond effectively to major changes in the education system, including changes in curriculum, teaching methodologies, assessment, school organisation and management, and to provide for teachers' personal and professional development needs. Ideally, the school climate should be one which welcomes and seeks to manage change and which exemplifies to students how change can be implemented and managed.

One of the crucial determinants of the quality of education is the quality of the individual and collective interaction between students and teachers, ranging from pre-school to adult and continuing education. Therefore, building the capacity of the education system to cope with and lead change is critically dependent on developing the necessary attitudinal and professional competencies in the teaching profession. The **Report on the National Education Convention** concluded: *"In the context of widescale curricular reforms, very changed participation patterns and new roles for schools, it was agreed that a sine qua non was provision for the in-career development of teachers, following from good initial education and teacher induction experiences"* (p. 135).

The professional developmental needs of teachers have increased sharply in recent years, in accordance with major educational and social changes. It is likely that these needs will continue and intensify in the future. The proposed curriculum revision at primary level, coupled with major changes in the senior cycle in second-level schools are obvious examples of this. Further examples are the importance of developing and disseminating more diversified teaching strategies to help combat educational disadvantage and to develop to their fullest potential those students with special needs. Moreover, the increased emphasis on collective school planning processes further underlines the importance of teachers developing new skills and approaches.

The major changes arising from increased devolution to schools, the critical role for boards of management in the operation of all schools, and more structured links with parents and the community, create important training needs for teachers, boards of management and parents.

In order to implement a major programme of development and training, the Government, with the assistance of the European Union, is committed to an expenditure of almost £40 million for in-career development from 1994 to 1999.

Present Position

At present a diverse range of activities is being undertaken involving numerous different organisations and groups which operate independently and often without reference to each other. While there is some very good work being done, frequent criticisms are that much of the provision is fragmented and that teacher participation is voluntary. In-career professional development is largely provider-driven, with decisions on priorities and the content of courses being made by the providers, usually in response to perceived needs. Providers include the universities, colleges of education, teachers' centres, teachers' unions, subject associations, the Department of Education, the Department of Health, and summer course organisers. Future policy will ensure that the systematically identified needs of participants – teachers, parents, and boards of management – will be the primary influence in determining the aims and the content of programmes.

An Approach to Policy

As with other professions, teachers have a personal responsibility to keep themselves abreast of new developments in their profession. They also should be afforded opportunities to participate in structured in-career training. Teacher education is a continuum in which quality initial training and well-managed structured induction are followed by well-devised in-career training programmes, available periodically throughout a teacher's career.

Both in the literature and among many providers, there is a consensus that an effective and comprehensive programme of professional and personal development for teachers requires a diverse range of measures and a variety of providers. Additionally, the strong message emerging consistently from all quarters is that the approach to professional and personal development should be decentralised, school-focused and conducive to high levels of teacher participation in all aspects of the process. This is not to say that there is no role for programmes and courses external to the school, nor for actions initiated by national bodies.

The approach to in-career development will be based on a centrally co-ordinated strategy, with an emphasis on the needs of schools and devolved arrangements for the provision of programmes. Education centres, will play a key role in planning and provision and in forming school clusters for in-career development. The **Report on the National Education Convention** stated that "*there should be a variety of forms of inservice teacher education, including an emphasis on school-based inservice provision. Inservice teacher education should take into account the personal and professional needs of the teacher, as well as those of the school system*" (p. 87).

The Department of Education will formulate, in active co-operation with the partners in education, a strategic framework for the in-career professional development of teachers with explicit, achievable objectives, specified target groups and criteria for evaluating the impact of in-career development programmes. Under this umbrella, the disparate elements of the present approach will be drawn together into a coherent strategy setting out priorities and associated budgetary allocations. The strategy will cover the following critical matters:

● the systematic identification of key objectives, priorities and target groups

● the manner in which training needs are identified, including the balance between school-based, regional and national needs

- criteria to assess the quality, relevance and cost-effectiveness of programmes required to meet the specified objectives and to facilitate the monitoring and evaluation of courses and programmes

- the establishment of criteria by which courses will be approved

- broad guidelines on modes of delivery encompassing the timing organisation, duration and structure of courses, including appropriate arrangements for the formal certification of courses

- appropriate continuity with pre-service education and induction training and taking account of the desirability of planned development over a number of years for individuals and groups

- criteria for the promotion of relevant research among teachers

- practical arrangements in relation to, for instance, substitution for teachers, travel and subsistence, and appropriate arrangements for study leave.

This strategic framework will provide the guidelines for schools and clusters of schools, as appropriate, to enable them to identify and respond to their particular needs. Structured staff development initiatives will be an important part of each school's approach to enhancing the quality of educational provision. The guidelines will also provide the framework for the education boards, and the education centres under their aegis, to formulate regional policies and approaches to cover issues of relevance to a range of schools and such as adult education and vocational education and training and to provide for the most cost-effective delivery arrangements.

Priorities for In-Career Development

The fundamental objective of the national in-career development strategy will be systematically to support changes in the education system to meet identified and emerging needs. A number of issues are particularly important in order to achieve effective change in the education system. Some of these are set out below.

School principals are key personnel and there is a need for specially targeted programmes for principals in both first- and second-level schools. One target is that, **by the end of the decade, all school principals will have participated in, and be part of, development programmes**. Specific courses will also be developed for middle management and for school planning. These will facilitate the more effective running of schools, improve the provision of educational programmes and facilitate the identification of performance targets against which to measure the achievement of educational objectives.

The major **curricular changes** in primary education, the continuing development of the junior cycle and the radical restructuring of the senior cycle, including the development of the transition year and new Leaving Certificate, will also be priorities for in-career development programmes.

There is a need for the provision of sustained high-quality in-career development programmes in the creative and performing arts to encourage curriculum leadership at primary level and to foster the unique and distinctive contribution of the creative and performing arts to the second-level curriculum. Curriculum development in art, music, dance, drama and media studies calls for such a sustained programme.

Similarly, the development of a new science programme as an integral part of the review of the social and environmental programme at primary level, and the continuing review by the National Council for Curriculum and Assessment of scientific and technological subjects at second level, imply a particular focus on teacher in-career development in science and technology.

In-career development priorities will also take account of the increased oral emphasis on the Irish language and on modern continental languages.

The identification of **students with learning difficulties** and special needs requires programmes to enable teachers to assist all students fulfil their potential. The particular training needs arising from the initiative in relation to pre-schooling will also receive special attention.

Course modules on **gender equality** will be an important feature in all in-career development programmes. Specific emphasis will be placed on combating sexual stereotyping and ensuring that the manner in which programmes are taught does not unwittingly reinforce gender bias.

The promotion of **more collegiality and co-operation among teachers** in schools in the development of whole-school approaches to educational provision and school planning, including the identification of curriculum leaders in particular specialisations, will be a particular emphasis of school-based in-career development.

In addition, the special needs of teachers and tutors working on **adult education and literacy programmes, vocational education and training programmes and Youthreach and traveller education programmes** will be a priority.

Development Programmes for Parents and Boards of Management

A central feature of the reform of the education system is the empowerment of boards of management and parents to take greater responsibility for the quality of educational provision in the school and for the promotion of closer co-operation between the school and the wider community. The ***Report on the National Education Convention*** recorded that it would be necessary "*to improve greatly the training opportunities for those participating on Boards of Management. Extra support would be needed, particularly in areas of disadvantage, where parents could sometimes be alienated from schools or reluctant to get involved*" (p. 26).

A board of management, operating through the principal and senior staff, has responsibility for the professional staff of the school, for all the students, for the financial management of the school and for the quality of educational provision. These are complex and major responsibilities, usually undertaken voluntarily and in a spirit of service. On account of this, the provision of **development programmes for boards of management** and the wider body of parents will be a priority. Their objective will be to foster relationships, to build structures for sharing and negotiation and to examine the need for a climate of trust and partnership in each school, as well as responding to specific training needs. These programmes will also seek to promote shared understanding among the board of management, the community of parents and the school staff about their respective roles and responsibilities. The objective will be that all boards of management will have access to relevant development programmes, taking account, as appropriate, of the unique features of schools as learning environments and drawing upon best management practice generally.

Organisational Arrangements

The following organisational arrangements have been put in place to support the development of a comprehensive national approach to the in-career professional development of teachers and to provide for the active involvement of the partners in education in the process.

A National **In-Career Development Unit** has been established in the Department of Education. This unit is advised by two committees, one for primary and one for second-level issues, and representative of management bodies, teachers, providers and parents. A Policy Development Committee, composed of senior Departmental officials, oversees the work of the Unit.

The main functions of the In-Career Development Unit are to develop and formulate a comprehensive policy on in-career education for teachers at first and second levels, including teachers on programmes such as Youthreach, vocational education, and training and adult education. This unit will also be responsible for developing a framework of training for parents and boards of management.

The Unit will prepare an annual programme and budget, consult with agencies in the preparation of policies, allocate funds for programmes and produce regular reports. The unit will determine programmes, courses and activities to be recognised for the purposes of leave of absence, as well as determining eligibility of courses for various types of appropriate support funding. The unit will set national priorities and guidelines for local initiatives. It will also liaise with and advise education centres, university departments, colleges of education and other agencies on the in-career professional development of teachers.

When established, **each education board will provide for the development of a comprehensive in-career training programme in its area**. In accordance with nationally agreed guidelines, it will also be responsible for making arrangements for the effective and efficient provision of such education and training. Specific budgets for in-career provision will be allocated to the education boards on the basis of their programmes and needs.

There has been a substantial development of teacher centre provision over the past two years. **These will henceforth be called Education Centres**. A discrete budget has been provided for the next six years for the development of these centres. This will include a major building programme and the employment of full-time personnel in the majority of centres. The centres will provide a focus for development programmes for teachers, parents and boards of management. Following the establishment of the education boards, these centres will come under their authority. This will enable the education boards to develop the work of education centres and to plan for a more co-ordinated approach to the development of teachers, parents and boards of management and for the provision of resource material.

Monitoring and Review of Effectiveness

The Audit Unit of the Central Inspectorate, on behalf of the National In-Career Development Unit, will be responsible for evaluating the national strategy for in-career development. The views of participants will be a regular feature of the evaluation process and external reviews will be commissioned as appropriate. The Audit Unit will also evaluate the outcomes of the provision made by the board in each region. Each board, in turn, will be responsible for the rolling review/evaluation of the in-career programmes in its area, including the review of the approaches of individual schools in the context of whole-school inspection. **The programme of in-career development will also be subject to annual review** by the relevant monitoring committee, set up under the arrangements for the evaluating the effectiveness of European Structural Fund expenditure.

Conditions of Service of Teachers

Policy Directions

The continuing changes in the education system, coupled with the major reform proposals outlined in this White Paper, present major challenges to teachers and management. Significant changes will be required to achieve the objective of improved school effectiveness. Teachers are of central importance in the education system; the quality of the system hinges on their competence and commitment. A number of important initiatives to enhance teachers' effectiveness and their professional standing are set out in this White Paper, including proposals in relation to pre-service education, in-career development, the establishment of a Teaching Council, the restructuring of posts of responsibility, the introduction of comprehensive school planning processes, the development of a Teacher Welfare service and agreed systems for appraising teachers.

Providing education, which is responsive to the demands of ever-accelerating change, requires teachers who are adaptable and reflective practitioners and who have the knowledge, skills and attitudes necessary to facilitate learning. Conditions of service crucially influence the morale and motivation of teachers, the effectiveness of schools, and the extent to which key policy targets in this White Paper will be realised. These targets include:

- the new curricular objectives at both first and second levels and the associated assessment strategies

- increased partnership with parents

- greater collegiality and accountability within schools, particularly in the context of whole-school planning processes

- restructuring posts of responsibility, including appointment procedures

- the targeted deployment of resources to areas of greatest need

- ensuring the integrity of the school day and school year

- greater teacher mobility and flexibility in the deployment of teachers, in the context, for example, of demographic changes curricular needs and changing patterns of school size

- quality assurance processes within schools, including teacher appraisal, the increased accountability of schools for the achievement of educational objectives and the development of appropriate performance measures.

Changes in conditions of service will continue to be subject to the agreement of the parties concerned. In future, the development of a unified and cohesive teaching profession will be promoted by extending the Teachers' Conciliation and Arbitration Scheme to include the conditions of service of teachers. Conditions of service will be negotiated through the Conciliation Council. Accordingly, **conditions of service for all teachers will, be considered, in future, in conjunction with salary provisions**. Procedures and arrangements for dealing with pay claims and changes in conditions of service for teachers will be set in the context of nationally agreed procedures and will be consistent with Government fiscal and pay policy. In the short term, the ***Programme for Competitiveness and Work*** will provide this context.

Schemes of job-sharing and career breaks will be developed further in consultation with management and teacher interests.

North/South Mobility of Teachers

The improved mobility of teachers within the island of Ireland has a potentially significant contribution to make to promoting enhanced mutual understanding among the traditions on the island. A priority will be to ensure, in consultation with all interested parties, that teacher mobility between both parts of Ireland is facilitated to the greatest extent possible. In this connection, one of the issues that will need to be examined is the question of the Irish language qualification for teachers who have received their training in Northern Ireland.

Appraisal of Teachers

Hitherto, the inspectorate of the Department of Education was heavily involved in the routine appraisal of teachers, particularly in the case of primary schools. In other countries, there is a growing emphasis on school-based appraisal systems. In the context of greater devolution, **schools in future will develop teacher appraisal systems within a nationally agreed framework**. In most cases, an appraisal system in effect will be a system for affirming good teachers, identifying strengths which would contribute to improved school performance and providing opportunities for personal and professional development.

A formal scheme for the systematic appraisal of school and staff performance does not operate in many schools. Therefore, **a policy objective will be to secure agreement in principle by management and teachers for the introduction of a school-based appraisal scheme**.

Unsatisfactory Teaching

The vast majority of teachers operate to high professional standards. However, there are a limited number of teachers whose performance is unsatisfactory. With regard to unsatisfactory teachers, the ***Report on the National Education Convention*** recorded agreement that "*the procedures for dealing with this issue were inadequate and that relevant support services for these teachers were not readily available*" and that there was "*considerable frustration among the public at large, as reflected in the contributions of the parent organisations, at the lack of progress in this area. This problem requires immediate attention*" (p. 43).

In considering this issue, it is important to recognise that poor performance by some practitioners is a problem facing all organisations and professions and is not one that is unique to the teaching profession. Under-performance can be defined as a persistent failure to achieve acceptable teaching and learning standards in the classroom.

The early identification of under-performance necessitates the appraisal of teachers' work. The initial identification of teachers experiencing professional difficulties should arise naturally, in the context of the appraisal of schools and teachers' work, carried out internally at school level.

When these teachers have been identified, it will be important to have available support services to which teachers can have access or be referred. In-career development provision is being increased to meet training needs. The development of a teacher welfare/counselling service will provide support to teachers who are experiencing a range of difficulties within and outside the school.

The Government is committed to establishing a comprehensive welfare service for teachers. A working party, consisting of representatives of management and teachers at first and second levels and the Department, has been set up to bring forward proposals for establishing a welfare service for teachers.

The number of teachers whose performance is such as to warrant the early retirement or removal from the system is quite small. However, this small group, can have a seriously detrimental effect on generations of students, can cause frustration to parents, colleagues and management alike and can reflect unfavourably on the image of the teaching profession. **Where unsatisfactory teaching performance is established as irremediable, it is necessary to remove the teachers concerned from the service**. There is a necessity to ensure that these teachers are dealt with fairly and that their rights are protected in accordance with agreed procedures, while ensuring that the detrimental effect of inadequate teaching on children is remedied.

Pending the introduction of appraisal schemes for teachers, the procedures for the identification, remediation and, if necessary, removal of under-performing teachers and principals, including agreeing a reasonable timescale for each stage of the process, are at present the subject of discussions with the concerned interests.

A Teaching Council

Rationale and Way Forward

The **Report on the National Education Convention** stated that "*The general view was that such a [Teaching] Council was timely in Irish circumstances and would give the teaching profession a degree of control over and responsibility for its own profession and allow for its closer engagement in the process of change*"

(p. 90).

The establishment of a Teaching Council would emphasise and enhance teaching as a profession. It has also been advocated that the role currently discharged by the Secondary Teachers' Registration Council should be extended to cover all teachers. Such a council would also act as the "competent national authority" for the implementation of the relevant European Union directive in relation to the mutual recognition of teacher training qualifications.

The establishment of a Teaching Council raises complex issues. These include the constitutional and contractual implications of compulsory registration for serving and future teachers, annual registration fees and disciplinary procedures, including deregistration. Consideration of these issues requires a balancing of the rights of individuals against the common good. The Convention Secretariat concluded "*that the legal issues . . . involved should be examined openly, carefully and comprehensively by the education partners, with a view to resolution*" (p. 90).

Following completion of consultation with the concerned interests and the resolution of outstanding legal difficulties, **the Minister will publish a draft legislative framework for the operation of the Council which will subsume the existing Secondary Teachers' Registration Council**. The framework will also set out the legal and policy issues involved in setting up the Council and a suggested response to them.

Remit and Composition of a Teaching Council

The functions of a Teaching Council include:

- establishing a register for all teachers

- laying down the conditions for registration

- following completion of the agreed procedures at school and regional level, administering disciplinary and deregistration procedures, including the conducting of enquiries

- offering advice on relevant policy matters, for example, teacher supply and demand, pre-service education, induction processes and in-career development.

The role of the Council will be to set and maintain the highest professional standards in the interests of teachers, students, their parents and the wider community.

The Teaching Council will encompass in its membership all teachers at first and second levels, thus emphasising the unity of the profession. Registration will be compulsory and the Council will be self-financing.

Since it will be a professional body representing the teaching profession, it seems appropriate that a majority of the Council be registered teachers. The Council will also include representatives of the other partners in education. The Minister will appoint an independent chairperson to the Council.

When bringing forward specific proposals, the Minister will set out definitively the functions, remit and composition of the Council. The Minister will also set out the appropriate relationship between the Council and schools, the education boards and the Department. In this context, the respective rights and responsibilities of the various bodies, in particular in relation to quality control and disciplinary procedures, will be specified. The Council will have wide ranging powers in matters of teacher discipline and recognition. It is not the intention that the Teaching Council should intrude upon the management responsibilities of boards of management or of the education boards.

Part

4

Parental Involvement

9 Role of Parents

The Constitution acknowledges that the primary and natural educator of the child is the family: article 42.1 states that parents have the inalienable right and duty *"to provide, according to their means, for the religious and moral, intellectual, physical and social education of their children"*. Children's first educational experiences are in the home, where the dominant influence is that of the parents. By the time the child enters school, the home has made a contribution to her/his development which will significantly affect the child's subsequent performance in the school.

Although most parents choose to avail of the expertise and resources of formal schooling, the role of the family in the child's development is crucial. Furthermore, the parents bring to the child's education the unique expertise derived from their intimate knowledge of the child's development, and their knowledge of particular needs and interests and circumstances outside the school.

Parents' role confers on them the right to active participation in the child's education. This includes their right as individuals to be consulted and informed on all aspects of their child's education at school level, and their right as a group to actively participate in the education system at school, regional and national levels.

Parents are integral partners in the education of their children. They will be consulted, as other recognised key interests are, and will have an opportunity to influence national educational policy and its local implementation. Parents also have responsibilities, including supporting the child's education, nurturing a learning environment and co-operating with the school in identifying learning needs and interests. Irrespective of socio-economic background, parental interest and attitude have a positive impact on children's learning where there is parental participation in the learning process and active participation with the teaching staff.

Relationships between the school and the home are of fundamental importance and this has been increasingly stressed in Irish educational debate. There is continuing evidence of a desire on the part of parents and teachers to develop and foster constructive co-operation. As part of national education policy, it is essential, therefore, to adopt a range of measures aimed at fostering active parental partnership with schools.

Partnership in Educational Management

In his concluding comments to the National Education Convention, the Secretary General stated *"I think that the Convention represents a distinctive landmark in relation to them [parents and communities]. I believe that their central-stage place has become more assured and that many productive linkages can be forged which will give new emphases to the education system"* (**Report**, p. 239).

The Government is committed to promoting the active participation of parents at every level of the education process. It also supports the right of parents to be consulted, as part of a collaborative process for educational decision making and policy making at school, regional and national level.

At national level, the National Parents' Council is formally recognised as the representative body for parents at first and second levels. Parents are full partners in the consultative process between the Minister, the Department and the other partners in education. **This formal recognition will be given statutory confirmation**.

Parents will be given a **statutory entitlement to representation** on each school board of management and each education board. In addition, as part of general guidelines in relation to selection procedures for school staff, which will be formulated by the Minister for Education, provision will be made for **parental involvement in staff selection** through their representation on selection boards. Consultation will be held with the national bodies representing the partners in education on this issue.

Individual parents and the collective body of parents have a central role to play in each school. A parents' association in the school is an important means by which the collective parental partnership in schools can be facilitated. A parents' association can provide structured support to parents, school staff and to management. **A statutory duty will be placed on boards of management to promote the setting up by parents of a parents' association** in every school in receipt of Exchequer funding. National guidelines will be developed, in consultation with the relevant interests, about the role of parents' associations, with the objective of ensuring the maximum contribution of parents to the life of the school. In turn, the role of each particular parents' association will be set out in the school plan, in collaboration with the parents' association.

Home-School Links

The role of parents in the home is crucial in forming the child's learning environment by promoting positive attitudes towards education, by encouragement and the fostering of self-esteem and by direct instruction relevant to the child's age and learning needs, such as reading activities and homework supervision.

It is very important, therefore, to develop dynamic and supportive links between the home and the school. As part of its school plan, **each board of management will be required to develop a formal home-school links policy**, outlining the school's approach to links with the home and with the general body of parents, and stating the actions which will be taken to foster such links. The home-school links policy will be formulated in consultation with the parents' association. This policy will include initiatives aimed at raising awareness of the parents' role in facilitating the child's learning, with particular advice on homework. The policy will also provide for sharing information, for continuing advice and for guidance on specific ways to enhance the learning process, the provision of information and training in relevant instructional skills and the provision of formal educational and training programmes for parents.

The policy will provide for joint training for parents and teachers to assist them in working together. The policy will also provide for a regular flow of information on the child's progress in school through parent-teacher meetings, school reports and individual consultation with teachers. Access to information by parents about the school programme and ethos will be made easier, as is already the case in many schools, through pre-entry meetings, class meetings, school handbooks, and the annual report of boards of management. **Boards of management will be obliged by statute to provide access by parents to records relating to their own children**.

Teachers have welcomed the greater involvement of parents in schools; they appreciate parents as important partners in the education of their children. The development and management of collaboration between parents and teachers in the educational progress of students, on the basis of mutual respect for one another's roles and responsibilities, is a powerful means of enhancing the value of education and schooling.

Measures for the Disadvantaged

Given that those most disadvantaged in society are least able to exercise their rights as parents, measures directed specifically towards disadvantaged communities are necessary to avoid increasing the gap of inequality through socio-economic differences. In this respect, the Minister intends to **continue and further develop the Home-School Links programme in areas of disadvantage,** as resources permit.

This programme approaches the prevention of educational disadvantage and parent-school collaboration through a range of initiatives including:

- local co-ordinators
- home visits
- additional school facilities
- parents' education through courses and classes
- teacher education in relation to partnership.

The programme was recently evaluated and will be further developed following consideration of the evaluation report. The overall objective is to alleviate the effects of disadvantage through facilitating the full participation of parents in the education of their children at first and second levels.

The Role of Education Boards

Parents will play a major role in the regional planning and co-ordination process to be discharged by each education board. Their contribution will be ensured through **statutory representation on each board and through consultation with parents in each region**. Each education board will foster a dynamic partnership between schools, parents and the communities they serve. As part of this remit, specific initiatives will include:

- a range of supportive actions, including the identification and transfer of best practice concerning parental involvement in schools

- engaging in a consultative process with parents on school accommodation needs, including new schools, and the provision of specialist facilities

- the development of clear procedures, in consultation with parents and school authorities, for the resolution of disputes concerning issues which had been raised and not satisfactorily resolved at school level.

- the provision of support services for the parents of children with special needs, as part of its responsibility for the co-ordination of educational provision, including support services, for these children.

Part
5

Organisational Framework

10 The Governance of Schools

Context

The governance of schools has been the subject of extensive deliberation and discussion among the partners in education for a number of years. The issue of school governance was considered in detail at the National Education Convention. The ***Report on the National Education Convention*** stressed that the fundamental question in relation to the governance of schools is *"whether appropriate adjustments and adaptations can be made to bring the governance of schools into line with very changed economic, social and political circumstances, while respecting the rights of various involved parties and winning the allegiance of the relevant partners within school communities"* (p. 23).

In July 1994, the Minister for Education issued a position paper on the governance of schools. The paper was considered in detail at a two-day meeting which was attended by the concerned interests in September 1994. Following that meeting, further discussions took place between the parent, teacher and management organisations at primary level. General agreement has now been reached on a governance model for primary schools, subject to agreement being reached on a model deed of trust, which will provide a legal basis for guaranteeing the specific ethos of each school.

Approach to Policy

The policy approach to the governance of schools outlined in this White Paper is based on the following considerations:

● governance structures for schools should respond to the diversity of school types, ownership and management structures which is a central feature of the structure of Irish education at primary and second levels

● governance structures should reflect the plurality of Irish society, including the rights and needs of minority groups

● the composition of boards of management should reflect and promote participation and partnership in the running of schools among patrons/ trustees/ owners/ governors, parents, teachers and the wider community

● the composition and operation of boards of management should reflect and promote public accountability to the immediate community served by the school and to the State as the predominant source of funding for schools.

The maintenance and promotion of a distinctive ethos and set of values for individual schools is supported by a strong societal consensus. This is a central concern for the majority of parents and for those to whom parents have entrusted the education of their children. In this regard, governance structures will be put in place in a manner which protects the rights, values and beliefs of parents, while promoting pluralism, partnership and accountability at the same time. Governance structures for schools will be developed within the following framework of responsibilities:

- the recognition of the responsibility of patrons/ trustees/ owners/ governors to maintain and promote a distinctive ethos in their schools and to ensure the practical means to discharge this responsibility

- the entrusting to boards of management of responsibility for the management and provision of education in schools

- the responsibility of the school principal and staff for the day-to-day achievement of the objectives of each school.

The policy objective, underpinned by legislation, will be to ensure that boards of management are established in all first- and second-level schools in receipt of Exchequer funding, in accordance with the foregoing principles.

Patrons/ Trustees/ Owners/ Governors

The functions carried out by patrons/ trustees/ owners/ governors differ between sectors and schools. In addition, a variety of arrangements exists between schools in regard to beneficial ownership and the control of schools within the terms of leases, trusts or other legal situations. In virtually all cases, the functions of patrons/ trustees/ owners/ governors relate to the original promoters and founders of schools, the most important of which is ensuring the continuity of the ethos of the school concerned, including a distinctive religious ethos.

Boards of Management

The essential function of a board of management will be to ensure **effective educational management and provision** in a school. A board will provide a management and support structure which will enable the principal and staff to achieve the aims and objectives of the school, on a day-to-day basis. A board will ensure the accountability of the school to parents and to students as well as to the education boards and the Department of Education. A board will carry out these functions within the overall framework determined by the patrons/ trustees/ owners/ governors and by education boards and the Department of Education.

A board of management will have a **statutory obligation** to ensure, through the principal and the teaching staff, that:

● the needs of students, individually and collectively are identified and responded to by the school

● school plans, agreed by the patrons/ trustees/ owners/ governors, are developed, implemented and regularly evaluated

● the curriculum, assessment and general education provisions within the schools are of a high quality and meet the requirements prescribed by the Department of Education

● management and staff development needs are identified and provided, within available resources

● procedures are in place through which parents can receive full information on all aspects of their children's educational progress, including access to their children's records

● the school complies with all the rules and regulations prescribed by the Department of Education.

A board, on behalf of the patrons/ trustees/ owners/ governors, will be responsible for **protecting and promoting the ethos of schools** as reflected in the desires and choices made by parents for their children. A board will strike a balance between the rights, obligations and choices of the majority of parents and students who subscribe to the ethos of a school and those of a minority who may not subscribe to that ethos but who do not have the option, for practical reasons, to select a school which reflects their particular choices.

A board will normally be the **legal employer of teachers**, while allowing for the continuance of existing arrangements, for the appointment and employment of teachers, where these already exist – for instance, in regard to the Vocational Education Committee schools or in a school where the employer is a board of governors. The board of management will be responsible for the appointment of all teaching staff in schools in accordance with the selection procedures sanctioned by the Department of Education, as outlined in Chapter 14 and subject to approval of the appointment, where required, by the patrons/ trustees/ owners/ governors. Boards will also have the authority to terminate teachers' contracts of employment, in accordance with prescribed rules and regulations and the relevant statutory requirements. This will be subject to the appeals provisions which are currently in place or which may subsequently be agreed.

The Way Forward – Primary

The continuing discussions on the governance of primary schools have led to substantial progress. A system of governance for primary schools, incorporating the agreed provisions outlined below, will be put in place when the terms of the model deed of trust have been agreed.

Term of Office

Boards of management will be appointed for a period of three years.

Structure of the Board

A "Core Board" be appointed consisting of:

- two nominees of the patron
- two parents elected from parents of students attending the school
- one staff member elected by the school staff
- the school principal, appointed *ex officio*.

The "Core Board" having discussed the responsibilities of the board, in line with agreed criteria, for the effective management of the school will propose two members from the wider community, agreed unanimously by the "Core Board" to the patrons for appointment.

Further discussions will take place in relation to the criteria for the nomination of the two members from the wider community. These criteria will include a commitment to the ethos of the school. These members will be in possession of skills complementary to the board's responsibilities, will have a commitment to education and its promotion and will contribute to the gender balance on the board.

The eight-member board will then be formally appointed by the patron, who will be responsible for ensuring a gender balance on the board.

A proportionate variation on this model will be necessary for one-teacher schools, while adhering to the principles set out above.

Chairperson of Board

The chairperson of the board will be appointed by the patron and will be a voting member of the board with a casting vote in the event of a tied vote. The issue of the appointment of the chairperson will be included in a general formal review, in relation to the governance of primary schools, after an agreed period.

Dissolution of the Board

The patron may, for stated reasons, dissolve the board of management, with the approval of the Minister for Education, if in the patron's opinion, the activities of the board of management represent a breach of trust and/ or represent a threat to, or a diminution of the ethos of the school. The Minister for Education may require the patron to make arrangements for the dissolution of a board and the appointment and election of a new board, where the board has failed to fulfil its responsibilities. These situations could arise, for example, in cases of financial irregularity. The provision for the dissolution of boards will be set out in legislation.

Transparency of Boards

Good management practice will determine the manner of reporting back to parents, staff and school community. In this respect, it should be agreed at each meeting of the board what may and may not be reported back by staff and parents' nominees. Board practice should facilitate and promote commitment by parents to the affairs of the school and the functioning of an effective parents' association. Each board will have a statutory obligation to promote the setting up of a parents' association in every school in receipt of Exchequer funding.

Second-Level Schools

The degree of accord and progress on governance structures achieved at primary level will provide a basis for discussion among the partners at second level, with a view to securing agreement on a structure or structures for boards of management in second-level schools. The discussions will be based on the considerations outlined in this White Paper, and will take account of the diversity of school types and management/governance structures at this level.

11 In-School Management

Introduction

Effective management and leadership at all levels within the school are essential if the school's goals are to be met. The achievement of school effectiveness depends crucially on the leadership offered by experienced and skilled principals, supported by vice-principals and post-holders.

However competent a principal may be as an administrator or as an organiser, s/he will not succeed without involving other staff in delegated leadership roles. It is increasingly common practice, particularly in large schools, for other teachers to help set goals, to consider how these will be achieved and to monitor their achievement.

The Role of the Principal

Schools are complex institutions. The manner in which the principal discharges her/his responsibilities significantly influences the effectiveness of the education provided in the school. As the ***Report on the National Education Convention*** stated *"In practice, direct day-to-day responsibility for the smooth and efficient running of the school is vested by the Board of Management in the principal. The principal is supported in this task by the vice-principal and the post of responsibility holders"* (p. 42). Under the direction of the board of management, the principal is responsible for determining the school's educational aims, formulating strategies to achieve them, encouraging the staff to support those aims, and developing the school's curriculum policies.

Good leadership is one of the key characteristics of successful schools. The ***Report on the National Education Convention*** noted that *"Research has identified a strong relationship between positive school leadership and institutional effectiveness, and describes the successful principal as providing skilled instructional leadership for the staff, creating a supportive school climate, with particular emphasis on the curriculum and teaching and directed towards maximising academic learning, having clear goals and high expectations for staff and students, establishing good systems for monitoring student performance and achievement, promoting on-going staff development and inservice, and encouraging strong parental involvement and identification with, and support for the goals of the school"* (p. 42).

Principals decisively influence the effectiveness of the school. The principal is central to shaping the aims of the school and to creating the supporting structures which promote the achievement of those aims. This underlines the crucial importance of the principal's instructional leadership role. She or he facilitates the creation of a high-quality learning environment and mobilises staff, individually and collectively, to establish educational objectives, to support their continuous achievement and to evaluate and learn continuously from experience.

Principals are expected to be familiar with every domain of the school's activities, including the work in the classroom, but, on their appointment, they often may not be adequately prepared for their task. As part of the expanded in-career development programme, principals will have available to them, on their appointment, **induction programmes** which will tackle specific areas of management, including staff management, as well as practical issues related to school administration. Education boards will have a particular responsibility for organising induction programmes which will include a **mentoring scheme**, whereby newly appointed principals will be paired with established and experienced practitioners, who will be available to advise them as necessary.

Throughout their careers, principals in all schools will have access to courses on leadership and management, especially those aspects relating to the management of staff and school leadership. Particular attention will be given to supporting principals to help underperforming and underachieving teachers in their work. A policy objective will be that, **over the next five years, each principal will have participated in a special in-career development programme** related to the role and functions of the school principal.

In addition to these courses, a further objective will be to establish formal **networks of principals**. The aim of these networks will be to provide mutual support, to promote the transfer of good practice among schools and to identify continuing training needs. The education centres, under the remit of the education boards, will facilitate the operation of these networks. Such networks will also be a valuable mechanism for identifying the most effective means by which the education boards could provide professional and administrative support services to schools.

Principals of small schools who have full-time teaching duties have particular needs which will be taken into account. Some of these needs will be met by means of specially designed in-career development courses for such principals. The networks of principals referred to above will also be useful in helping principals in small schools to develop school planning processes and management procedures which suit their particular circumstances.

Appointment and Terms of Office

The principal will be selected on the basis of procedures prescribed by the Department of Education, following consultation with the relevant interests. The objective of such procedures will be to ensure the integrity of the process and the selection of the most suitable person for the job. Principals will be appointed by boards of management, subject to the approval of the patron/ trustees/ owners/ governors and the sanction of the education boards. This framework will be sufficiently flexible to allow for different arrangements, for instance, in regard to Vocational Education Committee schools or in schools where the employer is a board of governors.

Each newly appointed principal will serve a one-year probationary term. At the end of this period, the principal's appointment will be made permanent by the board of management, subject to a positive evaluation of the principal's performance by the board of management and a satisfactory recommendation, with reference to stated criteria, from the Regional Inspectorate. Discussions about the implementation of this proposal will take place with the relevant interests.

Under current arrangements, principals remain in their post until retirement age. The National Education Convention considered whether principals should hold office for a fixed term and the **Report** recorded that "*The proposal was seen as having many potential attractions, especially if, in the first instance, it could be introduced on a voluntary basis for principals seeking early retirement or wishing to return to full-time teaching*" (p. 46).

In the interests of mobility – perhaps the single most effective means of transferring 'best practice' from one school to another – career enhancement and the vitality of school leadership, **all new, non-teaching principals will be appointed for a maximum period of seven years**. At the end of this period, there will be a number of options for benefiting from the valuable experience of these school principals. For example, it will be open to them to reapply for the principalship or to apply for principalships of other schools or for positions in the education boards, the Regional and Central Inspectorates or the education centres. Alternatively, some principals may wish to resume full-time teaching duties. Discussions about implementing this proposal will be held with the relevant interests. These will include the salary, pension entitlements and seniority position of former principals returning to full-time teaching and the particular position of principals who carry a full teaching load. The discussions will also explore the possibility of facilitating the transfer on a voluntary basis to other duties of school principals who have been appointed under the existing arrangements.

Boards of management and principals in all schools, supported by the Regional Inspectorate, will have an important role to play in identifying potential candidates for leadership and management positions and affording them the opportunity to gain practical experience in a wide range of curricular and administrative duties. This experience will be supported by relevant in-career development courses. While this preparation should begin as early as possible after initial training, a unique opportunity arises in the case of post-holders and vice-principals in larger schools to broaden their range of skills and management experience.

Whereas all schools are complex institutions, they increase in complexity in accordance with the size and level of the school. The role of principal in a large second-level school is particularly challenging. While she or he is the day-to-day manager of activities, including curriculum development, the discrete elements of the curriculum depend to a great extent on the knowledge and commitment of post-holders with qualifications in the various disciplines. Teachers need to be assigned responsibilities for particular subjects or departments and to be appointed as programme co-ordinators for the increasing emphasis on cross-curricular studies. Notwithstanding the fact that the principal would not have an academic qualification in each subject, s/he would receive regular reports from those with specific responsibilities and must be recognised as having the final responsibilities for the in-school appraisal of all teachers.

Vice-Principals and Post-Holders

In a small school, while the principal's leadership may be sufficient to influence the whole school, in larger schools, the ability of the principal to delegate effectively to vice-principals and post-holders and to promote a strong sense of collegiality among other teachers is crucial to the school's success. Effective delegation, then, is an integral and essential part of the process of organising and running a school.

The vice-principal is the person who, under the direction of the principal, shares the duty of co-ordinating the work of all sections of the school. The vice-principal should be capable of discharging all the duties of the principal when the latter is absent. The vice-principal should have devolved responsibilities for specific sections of the school on a daily basis. The principal and vice-principal should be seen as a cohesive management unit.

The selection procedure for appointing a principal should also apply to a vice-principal and both should have access to similar and joint in-career development programmes.

Significant restructuring and redefinition of the duties and responsibilities of vice-principals and post-holders will be required in order to align these more closely to the management and instructional needs of schools.

The **Report on the National Education Convention** noted that *"The present structure governing posts of responsibility in the post-primary sector evolved historically in an unstructured manner, and, to a large degree, unrelated to the management needs of the schools"* (p. 47). The **Report** further noted that *"In conducting any review of the middle management system in the schools it will be important not to create the impression that the allocation of posts of responsibility to teachers is to be regarded as payment for seniority in the profession"* (p. 50). Suggestions for the reorganisation of the middle management system are also contained in the **Report**, which noted that *"Devising senior teacher posts which assign responsibility and accountability to teachers for the academic and pastoral programmes in the school would reduce considerably the workload of the principal. Were this to happen, the* *principal would have more time to concentrate on the central aspects of management generally associated with this role"* (pp. 52 – 53).

Discussions on a major reorganisation of the middle management system – vice-principals and post-holders – will be initiated with the concerned interests, in the context of the relevant provisions in the ***Programme for Competitiveness and Work***. The major objectives of this restructuring will be:

- matching the responsibilities of the posts more clearly to the central tasks of the school and the clear specification of responsibilities for various posts

- focusing on the provision of opportunities for teachers to assume responsibility in the school for instructional leadership, curriculum development, the management of staff and their development, and the academic and pastoral work of the school

- the establishment of selection procedures for vice-principals and post-holders, with the aim of ensuring that the most suitable people are appointed. Criteria will be matched more closely to the responsibilities attached to the position. In this regard the ***Report on the National Education Convention*** pointed out that *"The qualifications, experience and track record of applicants, rather than their seniority, would form the main criteria for appointment to posts"* (p. 52).

Conclusion

The changes set out have the potential to significantly enhance school effectiveness. The changes involve a major transformation in schools, in terms both of a school's organisation and its operating culture. Effective implementation will require sustained attention over time, as well as consultation with the relevant interests.

12 *The School Plan*

Purpose

Schools, in common with most organisations, can derive many benefits from engaging in a systematic planning process. Putting in place a formal planning and reporting procedure can greatly assist schools to implement and manage change and improve the quality of education being offered to students. This process of planning offers an excellent opportunity for engaging the board of management, the principal, staff and parents in a collaborative exercise aimed at defining the school's mission and putting in place policies which will determine the activities of the school. Staff can become involved in planning and teamwork by focusing on whole-school issues, thereby counteracting the isolation which teachers may experience in their own classrooms. Teacher development needs are identified when teachers draw up school plans and establish priorities; this also enables a more precise specification of their in-career training needs. Teachers and parents are empowered through the process of school planning and in this way critically influence the quality of education in the school.

Through their representation on the board of management, and through the school's parents' association, parents will be effective partners in the school planning process.

These and other important benefits of school planning were identified and discussed in the ***Report on the National Education Convention*** (pp. 58-59). The ***Report***, however, also identified some reservations and concerns that were expressed by participants at the Convention, which could reduce the value of the planning process. These included:

- the preparation of documents confined to general statements of school policy in relation to its main activities which could have minimal influence on school practice and quality improvement

- the widespread publication of planning documents which might give an incorrect impression of finality to the process and also reduce its value

- concern that the production of a final document might be used as a rigid accountability mechanism for evaluating schools; if this were to occur, the planning documents may not convey the realities of school, but rather become marketing devices.

Structure of School Plans

Arising from these concerns, the **Report on the National Education Convention** proposed a model for the development of school plans which consists of two components. "*The first component should comprise, what may be termed, the relatively permanent features of school policy. These would include such elements as the ethos, aims and objectives of the school, curriculum provision and allocation, approaches to teaching, learning and assessment, and policies on home/school/community liaison, homework, discipline and enrolment*" (p. 59). The **Report** suggested that this section of the school plan could be published as a separate document and that any revisions could be published annually. This document, which would be circulated widely, would help to inform parents and others about the school and its general policies.

The **Report** went on to recommend that "*The second component of the plan, which might be titled the development section, would be devoted to outlining and reporting on the specific planning priorities which the school was undertaking. The concept underpinning development plans is that each school would undertake, on an on-going basis, a limited number of small-scale development projects which the staff have identified as important priorities. These priorities for development would arise out of an internal evaluation of the school's policies and practices, covering both curricular and non-curricular areas*" (p. 59).

It is envisaged that such projects could be implemented over not more than two years. All staff members in the school need not be involved in implementing all projects at the same time. However, over a period of years all staff would all be engaged in specific developmental work. These development plans would be of a professional and technical nature and mainly of relevance to the staff and boards of management. They would not be published on a wide basis, although project reports concerning developments under way could be incorporated in the annual school report. Once a development plan has been successfully implemented, it could be incorporated into the general school plan as part of the policy statement of the school.

Development of School Plans

The concept of the school plan is now generally accepted at primary level where many schools have well-developed planning models. **Guidelines on the preparation of school plans for this sector will be circulated to all schools.** The introduction of the revised curriculum for this level will provide an opportunity for those schools which already have plans to revise and update them, as well as for extending this practice to all the other schools in this sector.

It will be the responsibility of boards of management to ensure that all primary schools have school plans. Boards will approve such plans, subject to the approval of the patron, in relation to matters concerning the school's values and ethos. In practice, most of the development work will be devolved to the principal and staff in the schools. Boards will publish the policy section of the school plan to inform parents and others about school policies.

The practice of developing school plans is less well advanced at second level. Guidelines, similar to those being prepared for primary schools, will be devised in consultation with the relevant organisations, and will be circulated to the schools. Thereafter, **all second-level schools will prepare plans**, as in the case of primary schools, subject to the approval of the patrons/ trustees/ owners/ governors in relation to matters concerning the school's values and ethos. Boards of management will publish the policy section of the school plan to inform parents and others about school policies.

As part of the professional in-career development programme for principals and staff, specific training and guidance in the development of school plans will be provided. In the first instance, this training will be focused on the needs of principals and senior staff, who will be expected to play a leading role in developing school plans. In particular, the school planning process will be an important theme of the principals' networks outlined in Chapter 11. This will facilitate a continuous development process, whereby experience is shared and the transfer of good practice made easier. Further assistance, in the form of advisory and back-up services, will also be made available to schools through education boards, education centres, colleges of education and university departments of education. School management will give particular emphasis to this theme at staff meetings, seminars and on staff days especially during the early development period.

The board of management will be responsible for producing each year a short report on the school's activities, outlining how various elements in the school plan were implemented. School plans will form an important basis for the preparation of annual reports, and will become a central focus for the conduct of whole-school inspections.

13 *The Role of Schools in Promoting the Social, Personal and Health Education of Students*

Schools actively influence all aspects of the growth and development of their students. This influence includes the school's environment and climate, its curriculum and its interaction with the community. The promotion of the social, personal and health education of students is a major concern of each school. Schools provide opportunities for students to learn basic personal and social skills, which will foster integrity, self-confidence and self-esteem while nurturing sensitivity to the feelings and rights of others. The attainment of these objectives for all students is influenced by the climate of the school and the classroom, by the organisation and teaching methods, by the school's approach to students' personal difficulties, and by the wider educational and spiritual values transmitted by the school.

The promotion of the social, personal and health education of students throughout their time in school is an integrated part of the school's educational policy. It should reflect the role of parents as the primary educators and the need for a continuing partnership between parents and schools. It should respect the personal identity and background of all students.

Planning for the Promotion of Health and Well-Being

The concept of the health-promoting school involves a positive approach to the promotion of social, personal and health education for students. The development of school plans will provide an opportunity for each school to outline a coherent programme of health promotion and well-being. The curricular reform being undertaken by the National Council for Curriculum and Assessment at primary and second levels will support this development; it includes programmes in social, personal and health education, encompassing relationships and sexuality education.

There are three main strands to the promotion of health and well-being in schools:

- school climate
- the involvement of parents and wider community
- positive interventions.

School Climate

The school climate arises from the specific ethos of a school. It reflects the relationships among all members of the school community, the school's code of behaviour, the extent to which all students are valued and the school's general environment. As part of the planning process, boards of management will be encouraged to review the degree to which their schools:

● promote self-esteem in all students

● develop good relationships between staff and students

● encourage staff in setting a good example for students in social, personal and health-related issues

● encourage staff to identify students at risk of abuse in any form and to ensure that the necessary follow-up action is taken.

Involvement of Parents and the Wider Community

The health-promoting school will work closely with parents, the wider community and all agencies concerned with the health and well-being of students and their families when developing and implementing programmes. This includes:

● consultation with parents on the development of school policy for the promotion of health and well-being and the provision of information for parents on the school's programmes in this regard

● enhancing parental involvement in the promotion of health and well-being, particularly in disadvantaged areas, through the home-school links programme

● co-operation with voluntary agencies in educational and health promotional initiatives relating to lifestyle-influenced diseases such as cancer, alcoholism, heart disease, sexually transmitted diseases and HIV/AIDS

● co-operation with agencies concerned with safety and the environment.

Positive interventions

At school level, these will include:

● a physical education programme, beginning at the early stages of primary education, which will promote the physical well-being of all students and which will be linked to education on hygiene and diet, where appropriate

● the development of a school policy on personal and social education in consultation with parents and staff

● the provision of a relationships and sexuality education programme beginning at the early stages of primary education and continued as appropriate to all levels of students, which would involve close co-operation with parents, support and complement the work of the home and in keeping with the ethos of the school. A circular has been issued to all schools setting out the parameters of the programme and the basis for future development

● ensuring in-career development, appropriate to the needs of the school.

At national level, these will include:

● co-operation with the health boards in the development of a systematic health screening programme

● the continuing development of the Stay Safe Programme and its extension to all schools

● the development of programmes relating to tobacco, alcohol and substance abuse and the promotion of healthy lifestyles.

Relationships within the School

Interpersonal relationships within schools, and the way in which the school community is encouraged to be involved in the school's operation, have a significant bearing on both student and teacher behaviour. Boards of management, principals and teachers will all play a crucial role in the formulation and development of a school's policy on behaviour.

Parents have an important part to play in the development of high standards of behaviour among students and schools are entitled to their support. Likewise, school policies should be developed in close consultation with parents, and with students where appropriate. In order to facilitate this consultation, **the board of management of each second-level school will be encouraged to promote the formation of a students' council**, which will work in collaboration with the staff and the parents' association. In recent years, many schools have formulated codes of behaviour or have amended existing codes. The Department of Education has also issued guidelines on school discipline and behaviour and on school bullying. In the context of the development of school plans, the Department will continue to encourage boards of management, teachers and parents, at both primary and second level, to co-operate fully in the **formulation, updating and implementation of policies on behaviour and bullying**. An action-oriented project is being commissioned by the Department to evaluate the effectiveness of present codes, identify best present practice and make recommendations, including appropriate strategies for co-operation among adjacent schools.

14 Establishment of Education Boards

Introduction

The **Report on the National Education Convention** noted that a considerable change of attitude towards intermediate education structures had taken place in recent years. The **Report** also highlighted the range of views which existed on the powers and functions which any intermediate structure might have and on their relationship with individual schools.

The Minister issued a position paper on regional education councils in March 1994. The paper proposed functions, powers and duties for new intermediate education structures. It also dealt with their geographic remit and composition. Multi-lateral discussions, among the concerned interests followed. The independent chairman and rapporteur presented a report on these discussions to the Minister. Therefore, the proposals on intermediate education structures, now to be titled Education Boards, derive from extensive process of consultation.

Overall Approach to the Policy Decisions

The rationale for education boards includes:

- a need for greater awareness of and sensitivity to the needs of local and regional communities in order to improve the quality, equality, efficiency, relevance and flexibility of delivery of all educational services

- the value of further involvement and empowerment of local and regional communities, in addition to their current and continuing involvement at school level

- the desirability of releasing the Department of Education from much of its current involvement in the detailed delivery of services to schools, in order to allow it concentrate on the development and monitoring of the education system at national level

- a realisation that the demands of educational provision cannot, in many instances, be met at the level of the individual school.

Arising from the rationale, the essential criteria for the establishment of education boards are:

- they should promote equality of access to participation in and benefit from education

- they should enhance the quality of education, lead to improvements in effectiveness, efficiency and integration of services, and have an operational objective to provide quality education services at the lowest achievable cost.

- they should function as an effective partnership between the Department of Education, the providers of education, parents and local community interests, including the business sector and locally elected representatives

- their activities should be consistent with and contribute to the realisation of overall national educational policy and objectives

- they should elicit a broad level of acceptance

- they should reflect the diversity within the school system and other providers of education

- they should contribute to enhancing transparency in decision making

- they should enhance the public accountability of the education system.

Intermediate structures have the capacity to provide a necessary and vital enhancement to education at primary and second level to vocational education and training and to adult and community education. The high degree of autonomy exercised by schools is one of the strengths of the Irish education system. However, individual schools (with the exception of those in the Vocational Education Committee sector) relate individually with the Department of Education in regard to detailed operational matters. This can give rise to functional inefficiencies for both schools and the Department itself. The ***Report on the National Education Convention*** noted a concern that "*The highly centralised character of educational administration has also fostered a culture of dependency with an over-reliance placed by institutions on the Department's role which may have resulted in a sapping of self-reliance and innovative approaches at local level*" (p. 15).

Decisions

The Government has decided that:

- **legislation will be presented to the Oireachtas providing for the establishment of education boards, which will also set out their functions and composition**

- following enactment of the legislation there will be a **phased transfer of functions** to the education boards

- after a period of five years there will be a **full independent evaluation** of the effectiveness of the boards

- there will be **legislative reform and rationalisation of the Vocational Education Committee system**.

Functions

Legislation will provide that education boards will have substantial **co-ordination and support service** functions. In carrying out these functions, the education boards will not impinge on areas of responsibility and discretion proper to individual school boards. The education boards will also have regard to existing structures, such as those set up by denominational and other voluntary groups and by the Vocational Education Committees.

The education boards will be the co-ordinating bodies for adult and continuing education, vocational education and training, and outdoor education centres in their regions. The education boards will channel Exchequer funding to Vocational Education Committees or to other providers of these services. The boards will also have a co-ordinating role in relation to publicly funded youth and sport activities.

Phased Development

There will be a phased transfer of functions to the education boards followed by an independent and full evaluation. The boards will be developed on a phased basis, as follows:

- enactment of legislation

- establishment of education boards on a statutory basis and the appointment of members

- statutory empowerment of the education boards to recruit core staff, including a director, and to prepare draft plans for educational delivery for their regions within the context of national policy. A key element in these plans will be a phased timetable, together with costings, for the taking on of functions by the education boards. This will precede any operational role

- Ministerial authority to proceed with implementation on the basis of approved plans

- independent evaluation after five years of operation.

Geographical Remit

There will be ten education boards. Their geographical remit will be as follows:

Region	Counties
Dublin City	Dublin City Borough
Dublin County	Fingal, South Dublin, Dún Laoghaire/Rathdown
Mid-East	Kildare, Wicklow
Midlands	Offaly, Longford, Westmeath, Laois
Mid-West	Clare, Limerick, Tipperary NR
North East	Cavan, Monaghan, Louth, Meath
North West	Donegal, Sligo, Leitrim
South East	Carlow, Kilkenny, Waterford, Wexford, Tipperary SR
South West	Cork, Kerry
West	Galway, Mayo, Roscommon

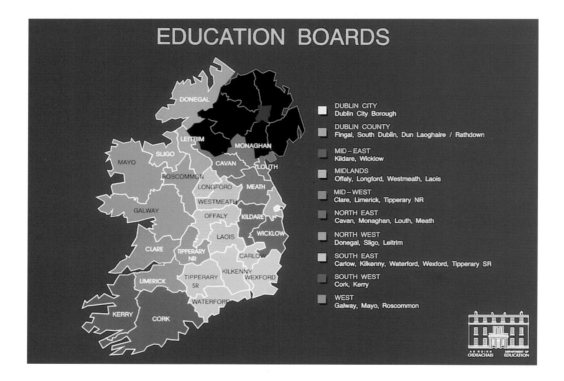

Composition

The board will be appointed by the Minister for a period of up to five years. The membership will be determined in a two-stage process.

First, a core board will be established, composed of:

● nominees from patrons/ trustees/ owners/ governors, including Vocational Education Committees, of which one shall be nominated by school managerial organisations

168

- parent nominees, nominated by the National Parents Council (Primary and Post-Primary)

- teacher nominees, of which one shall be nominated by school managerial organisations

- local elected representatives

- Ministerial nominees.

Second, the core board will put forward additional agreed nominees, exclusive of interests otherwise represented, for appointment by the Minister to the education board. These could be selected, as appropriate to each region, from the wider community and could include representatives of minorities and disadvantaged groups and people with special expertise. The additional nominees will be full and equal board members, sharing the same responsibilities and obligations.

Each of the constituent groupings will have equal representation on the boards, including the additional nominees put forward by the core board.

It is important to have a balanced representation of all involved interests on the education boards in order to underpin their acceptability and credibility among all those they serve, in their regions. Also, it is important that the total membership of the boards be set at a reasonable number in order to ensure effective operation.

The number of nominees, and the total membership, will also seek to provide for an appropriate balance of membership on the boards from the different local authority areas within the area of jurisdiction of a board, subject to an overall number of members consistent with effective operation.

The chairperson of the board will be elected by the members.

The precise numbers on the boards will be set out in legislation, which will also provide for an appropriate gender balance on all boards, in accordance with Government policy.

Specialist Committees

Each board will be empowered to establish committees and/or specialist groups to advise and assist it, as appropriate, in the implementation of policy. Such specialist committees will not normally be permanent, but will have a specific remit for a particular issue. Membership of the specialist committees will be drawn widely from the range of expertise and interests relevant to the subject area. The objective of such specialist committees will be to ensure maximum consultation with concerned interests, the provision of necessary expertise and maximum involvement of local communities and groups in the work of boards.

Operational Issues

Resource Implications

The **Report on the National Education Convention** stated that *"significant additional resources would be required in order to nurture a cultural climate which would enable the new structures to develop and gain the confidence of those they served"* (p. 21).

The establishment of the education boards will result in direct costs. Concern has been expressed throughout the debate that the education boards might become an expensive bureaucracy which would absorb resources needed by schools. For this reason one of the criteria by which the education boards will be evaluated will be that **any additional costs be outweighed by positive outcomes** and will enhance the effectiveness and efficiency of the overall system.

As further safeguards, the **funding of schools** will be protected by the provision of a separate budget line for school funding in education board budgets and by the publication of nationally determined criteria for the funding of schools.

The cost of education boards will represent a marginal additional cost rather than an entirely new area of expenditure. Some costs will be met by a **transfer of existing resources** to the boards in respect of functions which are already carried out by the Department or by Vocational Education Committees. The rationalisation of the Vocational Education Committee structure itself will release other current resources. The provision of additional support services to schools will require additional resources, whether provided by education boards or through some other agency. In this regard, the **Report on the Roundtable Discussions** noted that the alternative *"could be even greater costs in future years, since schools would (otherwise) not be able to respond to new needs or to cope with the problems building up in society"* (p. 22).

Staffing

Education board staff will be recruited by open competition through the Local Appointments Commission. The operational proposals put forward by education boards, as part of the process of phased development of their functions, may also involve the transfer or secondment of staff to the education boards from the Vocational Education Committees and the Department of Education. Negotiations will be held on any staffing arrangements involving the secondment or transfer of staff to the education boards. Ministerial approval for the operational functions of education boards will be contingent on there being agreement on all staffing issues, including transfers and secondments.

Funding

Education boards will receive annual grants from the Department in respect of their own activities. Ultimately, all Department aid towards the recurrent expenditure of first- and second-level schools will be made by way of a block grant to the education boards, subject to the retention of a centralised payroll. Recurrent expenditure covers teachers' pay, remuneration of non-teaching staff and non-pay elements. The current arrangements for funding non-pay expenditure involve capitation grants for national and voluntary secondary schools with separate arrangements for Protestant secondary schools, community and comprehensive schools and vocational schools. Funding of the remuneration of non-teaching staff involves a combination of meeting the costs of approved posts and allocating additional capitation grants.

In future, the allocation of standard resources for both non-teacher pay and non-pay would be made on the basis of nationally determined criteria. **Approved schools will have statutorily based entitlements to current funding** on the basis of these criteria. Additional funding will be made available to the education boards for the allocation of supplementary funds to schools and students based on nationally determined criteria, which would be so designed as to allow education boards to make allocations on the basis of locally determined priorities consistent with national criteria.

Grant aid in respect of **vocational schools** will be channelled through the education boards to Vocational Education Committees rather than to the individual vocational schools.

The central calculation and payment of the **Protestant Block Grant** will be retained to suit the special needs of second-level Protestant schools.

Funding mechanisms will be developed to ensure that all primary and non-fee-paying second-level schools will be funded on an **equitable and transparent basis**.

Common criteria and entitlements will apply to the funding of schools in the second-level sector. Currently voluntary secondary schools are funded on a *per capita* basis. Schools under the auspices of Vocational Education Committees are funded on a historic cost basis. Community and comprehensive schools are funded on an annual budget basis. **A steering group will be established** to draw up a recommended funding framework which would ensure equal treatment for different schools within this sector, while taking account of the needs of these different schools.

The membership of the steering group will include representatives of organisations representing patrons/ trustees/ owners/ governors, managements and teachers in the second-level sector as well as representatives of the Departments of Education and Finance. (The steering group will be assisted in its work by a working party of technical experts appointed by the Minister for Education). **The education board legislation will not be given effect until decisions had been taken by the Minister on the report of the steering group.**

Appointments in Schools

Boards of management will be responsible for the appointment of all teaching staff in schools, in accordance with the selection procedures sanctioned by the Department of Education. The objective of these selection procedures will be to ensure the integrity of the process and the selection of the most suitable teachers.

Appointment procedures will provide for approval of the appointment by the patrons/ trustees/ owners/ governors. Appointment procedures will also provide for sanction of appointments by the education boards. This framework will be sufficiently flexible to allow for the continuance of different arrangements, for example in regard to the Vocational Education Committee schools or in a school where the employer is a board of governors.

Each education board will introduce measures to ensure that, where Exchequer funds are used to fund teachers, approved selection procedures are being operated in a fair and reasonable manner and teachers of high quality will be recruited as a result. Boards of management will normally be the legal employers of teachers, although other arrangements will also be consistent with this framework (for example, Vocational Education Committee schools where teachers are employed by the committees, or schools where the employer is a board of governors).

Salary Payments

At present, the Department of Education pays the salary and allowances of all teachers in primary, secondary, community and comprehensive schools, while payment of salary to vocational teachers is the responsibility of the Vocational Education Committees. School authorities and Vocational Education Committees are also responsible for the payment of all non-teaching staff. It is intended to retain the centralised teacher payrolls for teachers.

Re-deployment of Teachers

Education boards will exercise the role currently exercised by the Department of Education in the operation of redeployment schemes and substitution panels.

Curricular Provision

As part of their co-ordinating and regulatory functions, education boards will be required to ensure the availability of as broad a range of options as possible to students within their areas of jurisdiction. This will be done through involvement in school rationalisation, through the education board's role as a provider of support services, by encouraging and facilitating inter-school co-operation in the most efficient use of specialist resources, particularly in relation to scientific and technological education, and by encouraging the development

172

of shared facilities for science, technology and the creative and performing arts. This will also include provision for the acquisition of advanced skills for those who demonstrate special talents for dance, or the playing of a musical instrument.

School Attendance

The School Attendance Act of 1926, and subsequent amendments to the Act, oblige parents to ensure that children attend school from age six up to age fifteen unless there is a reasonable excuse, for example, through illness, or where the child is receiving suitable elementary education, other than by attending a national or other suitable school. The provisions of the Act are enforced by School Attendance Committees in Dublin, Cork, Dún Laoghaire/ Rathdown and Waterford which employ school attendance officers and by An Garda Síochána outside these areas.

A task force has been established in the Department to:

● examine the submissions received from interested parties in response to the report on truancy issued by the Department in April 1994

● consider and make recommendations as to future action required to address the problem of truancy at first and second level.

At the same time, the process of reviewing the existing legislation in this area is currently under way in the Department. Taking account of these findings, the education boards will be given **statutory powers and responsibilities** in regard to the monitoring and enforcement of school attendance.

Accommodation

Education boards will have power to **own school buildings for leasing to different groups of patrons/ trustees/ owners/ governors, in order to provide for the specified educational needs of an area**. Buildings for new schools will be provided through this mechanism, which will also be available for use in conjunction with the procedures to be established for the rationalisation of school provision. This mechanism will allow for the establishment of a variety of school types, including denominational, multi-denominational and all-Irish schools. The type of school will be reflected in the terms of the lease. The criteria which will be employed for the leasing of school buildings will be established nationally and will be published by each education board.

Support Services

There was a broad measure of agreement at the Convention that intermediate structures could have a major role to play in the provision of support services to schools.

The education boards will be required to include proposals for such support services in their plans. These services will extend to members of boards of management, parents and non-teaching staff, as well as teachers. The extent of the services will have regard to the availability of resources and will be delivered within approved budgets.

While the extent and scope of the support services will depend on the resources available from Exchequer sources, ultimately, the support services to parents, boards of management and Vocational Education Committees will include:

- management services for schools
- industrial relations and legal services
- teacher welfare service
- curriculum support and staff advisory services
- school psychological service
- library and media service
- building maintenance service
- rationalisation and amalgamation services.

Accountability of the Education Board and the Respective Roles of the Board and the Director

Effective devolution requires clarification of the respective roles, powers and responsibilities of different organisational levels within the overall system. It needs:

- a policy and budgetary framework
- an accountability framework, with criteria for the discharge of roles at different levels
- a process within which to evaluate outcomes and procedures, so as to ensure compliance.

Provisions for the accountability of education boards will clarify the respective roles and responsibilities of the Minister and the Department, the education boards and boards of management. Social and public support for these provisions is important, not only for the better achievement of objectives within the education system, but also to secure resources for education as a priority within the many competing social demands which draw on public funds. Clear public perceptions of cost-effective spending on education will help to achieve this aim.

The Exchequer is virtually the exclusive source of public funding for education, in the absence of any significant funding of education through local taxation. **The Minister is accountable to the Dáil** for ensuring that Exchequer funds on education are spent on the programmes and activities for which they have been assigned, that expenditure remains within budget, that assets are adequately safeguarded and that high standards of economy, efficiency and effectiveness are reached and maintained.

While education boards, boards of management and other local or regional interests should act in accord with national policies and must comply with the requirements of financial accountability, the framework will also be empowering in order to permit regional and local flexibility within national guidelines.

The following structures and procedures will be provided for by the education board legislation:

- the policy framework and relevant guidelines will be determined at national level, following appropriate consultation. The policy framework and national guidelines will have due regard to local and regional flexibility and the needs and interests of minority groups

- there will be a phased transfer of functions to the education boards

- following consultation, each education board will be required to develop and submit to the Minister for approval a five-year educational plan for the educational provision in its area. The plan will be reviewed annually

- following consultation, each education board will be required to submit a one-year educational programme and budget consistent with the five-year plan for the approval of the Minister

- Exchequer funding will be paid to education boards in accordance with approved budgets. Separate budget lines will be identified for major programmes and schemes, including, for example, grant aid to schools

- all approved schools will have statutorily based entitlements to current funding on the basis of nationally determined criteria for both non-teacher pay and non-pay. Additional funding will be made available to the education boards for the allocation of supplementary funds to schools and students, which will be designed to allow boards to make allocations on the basis of locally determined priorities consistent with national criteria. The allocation of teaching posts will be made in line with nationally agreed ratios and criteria

- education boards will have flexibility to make adjustments to individual budget lines within their overall financial allocations. This will enhance the ability of boards to respond to local needs and priorities, but it will not impinge on the core funding entitlements of individual schools

- no expenditure will be incurred or commitments entered into by an education board except in accordance with an approved five-year plan and an approved annual programme and budget

- the Minister will be empowered to require an education board to desist from a particular activity which has not been approved and to require an board to engage in an activity which is within its overall remit

- education boards will be required to keep such records and accounts as may be specified by the Minister and to provide such information as may be required by the Minister from time to time

- education boards will be required to prepare annual financial and educational reports for submission to the Minister

- the accounts of education boards will be audited by the Comptroller and Auditor General

- provision will be built into legislation to ensure compliance by the education boards with the relevant legislation and with lawful and appropriate Ministerial instructions.

Within each education board, there will be a clear distinction between the role of the board and that of the Director. **This distinction arises from the need to separate the very different roles and responsibilities of the board members acting collectively from that of the Director, as head of the executive arm of the education board and as accounting officer.** The board will be responsible for the formulation of policy and for monitoring the implementation of policy. Accordingly, it will be the responsibility of the board to approve the five-year educational plan and the annual educational programmes and budgets for submission to the Minister for Education. The board will also be responsible for ensuring that the activities and actions of the Director and staff of the board are in accord with the plans, budgets and Ministerial directions as well as such other regulations and conditions as may be provided for in the legislation (for example, staff regulations).

In the case of the five-year educational plan and annual educational programme and budget:

- the Director will prepare draft proposals to reflect regional and local needs and priorities, national policy guidelines and the views and decisions of the board

- the board will approve the draft proposals with or without modification. Modifications will be made only after consultation with the Director

- the draft, as approved by the board, will be forwarded by the Director, acting on behalf of the board, to the Minister for approval

- the Director will be responsible for the implementation of the plans, programmes and budgets as approved by the Minister subject to oversight by the board

- the Director will be designated as the accounting officer for the education board and will be given statutory responsibility for budgetary and financial control, including ensuring that records and accounts are properly kept, that expenditure is in accordance with approved programmes and budgets and that appropriate controls are in place.

The Director, furthermore, will be the leader of the educational personnel in the area and the driving force behind the policy development and programme implementation by each education board.

Directors will be recruited by open competition, from the widest possible field covering all sectors of education and other relevant disciplines. Selection and appointment will be made through the Local Appointments Commission and on the basis of fixed-term contracts. The terms of appointment, conditions of service and remuneration will be subject to the approval of the Minister. The specifications for the post will include the statutory duties of accounting officer. Directors will report annually and publicly to the education boards and to the Minister on the discharge of their duties, including the operation of the appeals process, as outlined below.

Appeals

In the case of schools, the necessity for procedures to resolve disputes arise in a number of contexts, with staff, students and parents as potential appellants. Current mechanisms for resolving disputes include access to the courts, industrial relations processes and a variety of special appeals procedures including disciplinary procedures. Important features of appeals mechanisms include established process, clear grounds for appeal, independence from the original decision maker, safeguards against abuse through frivolous or mischievous appeals, speed and finality.

Existing mechanisms and procedures will be retained, but there is a potentially constructive appeal role for education boards in such areas as enrolment and discipline. In the first instance, most cases within these categories are capable of resolution within individual schools, by reference to the boards of management if necessary. However, in some instances, it will be desirable to provide an independent forum which can adjudicate on complaints.

It is intended that education boards will meet this need. To that end, they will develop clear procedures for the appeals process in consultation with parents and school authorities.

Reform of the Vocational Education Committee System

The retention of the Vocational Education Committee system, within the new education board structures, will be accompanied by legislative reform. This will necessitate **changes to the legislation under which the Vocational Education Committees operate**.

Changes have occurred since the 1930 legislation was enacted. The statutory framework and related financial controls were established at a time when the Vocational Education Committees received most of their revenue from local taxation. Now most of the funding, including European Union funds, comes through the Exchequer. The role of the Vocational Education Committees needs to be redefined *vis-a-vis* the education boards and other providers and in particular to ensure that all schools and providers in receipt of state funding will relate to the new structure on an equal basis.

The amending legislation for the Vocational Education Committees will provide for the retention of the Vocational Education Committees as statutory committees, with a substantial local authority involvement, with responsibility for:

- the second-level schools currently under their remit

- ownership of their schools

- employment of staff

- appointment of boards of management to their schools.

The legislation will also provide for the recognition of the Vocational Education Committees as providers in the following areas, in addition to the general junior-and senior-cycle programmes at second level:

- vocational education and training, including Post-Leaving-Certificate courses (See also Chapter 4 on the establishment of the Further Education Authority)

- adult and continuing education (See also Chapter 4 on the establishment of the Further Education Authority)

- outcentres

- the arts in education

- operation of outdoor education centres.

The Vocational Education Committees will function as providers of education within the framework established nationally by the Minister for Education and elaborated regionally by each education board. Other providers such as primary, community, comprehensive and voluntary secondary schools, voluntary organisations and community groupings will be free to be involved in these activities, subject to the necessary co-ordination and funding which at regional level will be the responsibility of the education boards. Exchequer funding and support of providers including the Vocational Education Committees other schools and voluntary and community organisations, will be channelled through the education boards.

The considerations applying to education boards in relation to effective devolution, accountability for exchequer funding, compliance with national policy and flexibility to meet local needs and choices, will apply also to the Vocational Education Committees. Consequently, the new system of financial controls for the Vocational Education Committees will follow a similar pattern to those of the education boards. Vocational Education Committees will be required to submit corresponding plans, programmes and budgets to the relevant education board for consideration and incorporation, with or without modification, into the plans, programme and budgets of the education boards. The plans, programmes and budgets approved by the Minister, will include the operation of the Vocational Education Committees. Vocational Education Committees will discharge their responsibilities within the approved programmes and budgets and will be subject to the similar provisions for monitoring and accounting.

The Rationalisation of the Number of Vocational Education Committees

An important factor in considering the geographic remit of the education boards was the need for a sufficiently large area to provide for the effective concentration, rather than a wide dispersal, of resources. This consideration also applies to the geographic remit of Vocational Education Committees. Judged by this criterion, the areas of jurisdiction of many of the existing Vocational Education Committees would appear to be too small to be cost effective. This applies in particular to the urban district Vocational Education Committees but extends also to some county Vocational Education Committees.

Consequently, legislation to amend the Vocational Education Acts will contain provision to allow for:

- rationalisation of Vocational Education Committee structures – this would be a gradual process to be undertaken as the education board framework is progressively put in place

- to provide for the selection of the Chief Executive Officer and non-teaching officers through the Local Appointments Commission

- to allow for the transfer of some staff from Vocational Education Committees to education boards where functions are transferred or spare capacity is shown to exist

- to provide for the payment of teachers employed in Vocational Education Committee schools through the central teacher payrolls operated by the Department of Education

- to make legislative provision to allow for the transfer of some staff between Vocational Education Committees as part of a rationalisation process.

It has been decided that a commission on school accommodation needs will be established to conduct comprehensive demographic and statistical research and to advise the Minister (see Chapters 2 and 3).

The first priority of this commission will be to examine the existing Vocational Education Committee structure, and to report and make recommendations on the rationalisation of Vocational Education Committees. The report and recommendations will be set in the context of the establishment, functions and responsibilities of the education boards. The commission will also have full regard to the key principles and policy aims set out in the White Paper.

The commission will report within three months of its establishment and its report will be published. The legislative rationalisation of Vocational Education Committees will be implemented in advance of the formal establishment of education boards, taking full account of the recommendations of the Commission.

15 The Role of the Inspectorate

The Inspectorate of the Department of Education plays an important role in relation to the operation and quality of the education system in the primary and second-level sectors. The inspectorate currently has the main responsibility at national level for quality assurance in these sectors. It is also concerned with the dissemination of good practice. Inspectors participate in a wide range of activities at school and at national levels and are actively involved in the operation and management of the national Certificate Examinations. At present the inspectorate is divided into three divisions – primary, second-level and psychological service/guidance respectively.

Major Issues

The role of the inspectorate was considered in detail at the National Education Convention. The **Report** acknowledged the important and unique role of the inspectorate in relation to enhancing the quality of primary and second-level education. At the Convention, there was general appreciation for the work of the inspectorate in supporting schools and teachers. This was coupled with apprehension about the implications of proposals that the inspectorate would withdraw from its traditional contact with schools.

The **Report on the National Education Convention** expressed concern about the capacity of boards of management and principals in schools, because of limited expertise and experiences, to take on major new responsibilities, especially in regard to quality assurance. The **Report** also expressed concerns about the potential and perceived conflicts between the advisory and evaluative roles of inspectors.

Decisions on the future organisational structure and operations of the inspectorate outlined in this chapter reflect these concerns. They are also consistent with the other major structural changes set out in this White Paper: the increased focus of the Department of Education on policy formulation and quality assurance, the establishment of education boards, the emphasis on the autonomy of schools, the strengthened role of school management, and the specific responsibility of boards of management and of the education boards for the provision and quality of services.

The New Structure

Previous discussions, including those at the Convention and the Roundtable on intermediate structures, had considered the issue of a two-tier inspectorate: a Central Inspectorate for the purpose of ensuring quality control and for educational evaluation at national level; and a Regional Inspectorate, responsible to an intermediate tier, with primary responsibility for providing advisory and support services to schools.

While the rationale underlying this concept meets a number of the concerns expressed above, it would dilute the role of the education boards in evaluating outcomes in their own regions. Moreover, it would not be an efficient use of the inspectorate.

There are approximately 170 inspectors and psychologists working in the Department of Education. It is important to ensure that this valuable and scarce resource is fully utilised. **The inspectorate will continue to be recruited nationally by the Department of Education**. Most inspectors, however, will be seconded to the education boards, to work under the executive direction and authority of the directors of these boards. These inspectors will constitute the **Regional Inspectorate**. A small number of inspectors (the **Central Inspectorate**) will be assigned to the Department of Education to support the policy, evaluative and executive functions of the Department. There will be career progression and mobility between these two streams within the inspectorate.

The Central Inspectorate

The Central Inspectorate will be organised within the Department of Education as a small cohesive unit, based on functional responsibilities. The primary purpose of the Central Inspectorate will be to establish, evaluate and promote the highest national standards of quality in educational provision. To achieve this purpose, the Central Inspectorate's core functions will be:

- to **evaluate** and report on the standards and quality of the education provided and the effectiveness of policies and their implementation (Evaluation Function)

- to **advise on policy** formulation (Policy Function)

- to **supervise the operation of the national examinations** system (Examinations Function).

The inspectorate will be reorganised into three units: an audit unit, a policy unit and an examinations unit, under the direction of the Chief Inspector.

The Evaluation Function of the Central Inspectorate

The Audit Unit of the Central Inspectorate will concentrate on evaluating and reporting on the **quality and effectiveness** of the provision of educational services at regional and national levels. It will carry out this function through:

- the preparation of reports on major curricular and other issues
- monitoring and advising on the quality of teacher pre-service, induction and in-career development programmes
- monitoring and evaluating the effectiveness and outcomes of the national examinations system
- systematic educational audits of the effectiveness of the education boards
- commissioning surveys of attainment in curricular areas.

This work will be carried out on the basis of **selective audits** and a limited number of **annual in-depth inspections of schools**. The purpose of these evaluations will be to provide information and data on overall educational outcomes and standards nationally and to provide benchmark national data for the evaluation programmes carried out by education boards.

The Policy Function of the Central Inspectorate

The Policy Unit of the Central Inspectorate, a small group of expert personnel, will play a key role in contributing to the formulation and development of **national educational policy** and in designing policy implementation strategies in support of the Strategic Policy and In-career Development Units of the Department. They will also be responsible for the professional input into the evaluation of policy priorities in all the major facets of education, including curriculum, teaching, assessment, special needs, pre-service education and in-career teacher development programmes, vocational education and training and adult and continuing education. In carrying out this task, they will also be responsible for ensuring that relevant **research** and international experience are taken account of in the policy formulation process and for commissioning specialist studies.

The Examinations Function of the Central Inspectorate

The role of the Examinations Unit of the Central Inspectorate will be to manage the professional and academic aspects of the operation of the national certificate examinations. It will continue to ensure that the examinations reflect the aims of the curriculum, and will also continue to monitor standards.

Annual Report

The Central Inspectorate, working under the direction of the Chief Inspector, will publish an annual report on the quality of education. In doing so, it will draw on reports prepared by each education board.

Regional Inspectorate

The **Report on the National Education Convention** recorded that *"there was general agreement that an intermediate educational tier could have a valuable role in supporting the quality of educational provision within the system"* (p. 19). However, the **Report on the Roundtable Discussions** on intermediate education structures recorded that an intermediate structure *"should have an advisory support service and a quality assurance role"* (p. 13).

A regional inspection function will be an important element in helping each education board to meet its responsibility for monitoring the quality of education in the primary and second-level schools in its area. The closer the inspection service is to schools, the more effective it is likely to be in establishing a constructive partnership with boards of management and parents in its region, in disseminating good practice and in identifying and quickly tackling problems.

Distinction between Advice and Evaluation

The organisation and structures of the Regional Inspectorate will distinguish clearly between the advisory and evaluative roles, as was recommended in the **Report on the National Education Convention**. In order to avoid the confusion which could arise if the two roles were carried out by the same individuals in regard to the same schools, arrangements will be made to ensure that individual inspectors or groups of inspectors do not carry out both functions in a particular school. In this regard, education boards will co-operate so that some whole-school and other inspections within their areas are carried out by inspectors assigned to another board.

The Advisory Function

The advisory function will include assisting school managements in relation to school planning, staff development initiatives and the identification of in-career needs. It also will include the provision of psychological services, the management of visiting teachers' services for children with special needs and other issues, such as the placement of students with special needs. These functions will be carried out by inspectors assigned from the Department of Education to the education boards and also by teachers on secondment to the education boards for fixed periods.

Each school will be assigned a named inspector, who will be the first point of contact between that school and the education board. The duties of this inspector in relation to these schools will be advisory. This inspector will not take part in the evaluations of the school carried out by other inspection teams consisting of other inspectors.

The Evaluation Function

The education boards, through the inspectors assigned to them, will be responsible for the evaluation and monitoring of the quality of education within schools in their regions.

Inspectors assigned to the boards will carry out in-depth inspections on a range of schools on a regular, cyclical basis. School inspection will take place within an agreed time frame, with a whole-school focus, and in co-operation with the school in the context of its school plan.

To ensure equitable evaluation, performance indicators and criteria will be developed at national level which will give consistency to the procedures used for inspecting and reporting at regional level. These indicators and criteria will be transparent and will be designed to facilitate fair and objective judgements on the effectiveness of each school. They will take account of initial entry standards of students to the school and the educational progress subsequently achieved.

The inspection criteria and performance indicators will be made clear to schools before an inspection begins, in order to ensure that the inspection will be carried out in partnership between schools and the inspectorate. Inspections will assess the quality and nature of the education provided by schools and the extent to which they are achieving their objectives as set out in their school plans. The underlying purpose will be to improve the quality of education in the schools and, in addition, to provide appropriate information to the community served by the school, school management and staff and the central and regional authorities. The inspection will take account of the information on the attainment of students which is available in the school and how they are performing in school. This information will include academic attainment, social development, out-of-school activities, general co-operation and all other measures introduced by the school to enhance learning.

The inspection process will evaluate and monitor student achievement, the deployment of staff, the quality of school buildings, the extent to which educational guidelines are being followed, the provision for remedial education and the manner in which all the resources of the school – human, physical and financial – are being used.

The Department of Education will publish draft proposals for consultation with the partners in education on the guidelines and code of practice for school inspections. Schools will be encouraged to participate in the evaluation of their own work by reference to the key objectives in the school plan. In addition, in order to reflect the strengths of the schools being inspected, the inspection process will also provide strategies for helping schools which may be experiencing difficulties. These strategies will be linked to appropriate in-career development for teachers. Inspectors will visit classrooms and will consider the work of individual teachers. The purpose of these visits will not be to provide reports on the individual teachers, but rather to complete the information available on the educational work being carried out in the schools. The team of inspectors will have discussions with the school management, the principal teacher and the senior staff, groups of teachers, the boards of managements and representatives of parents. These discussions will take place before, during and after the inspection. Inspection teams will also consult with those inspectors designated as advisors to the individual schools in order to ensure that the particular circumstances of each school are taken fully into account.

The inspectors' reports will identify strengths and weaknesses within each school. Where, during the normal cycle of inspection, particular schools are seen to need support, the inspectors will make follow-up visits to assist them. Where serious shortcomings are identified and reported, it will be a matter for the board of management and the school to adopt action plans to deal with these. **The inspectors will make recommendations for improvement to school management and to the education board, as appropriate**. Subsequent to the completion of the whole-school inspection, the Regional Inspectorate will be available to advise and support schools on implementing recommended changes.

Provision will also be made for a mediation and arbitration process where a school challenges inspectors' reports. This procedure will be carried out by the Central Inspectorate, whose decisions in the event of arbitration will be final.

Psychological Service/Guidance Inspectors

The *Report on the National Education Convention* acknowledged the key role for schools of the psychological and guidance services and recommended: "*In the context of a re-organised Department of Education and of the inspectorate, the role of the educational psychologist should also be incorporated as an integral part of new planning*" (p. 66). The *Report* acknowledged that, while the nature of the psychologist's role varies at primary and second levels, there seems to be a need for more emphasis on educational guidance at both levels and a greater integration of the work of psychologists and teachers.

The *Report* concluded that "*The psychological service ought to be developed as an integrated one for both primary and post-primary schools*" (p. 66). The *Report* also highlighted that, because many problems which become obvious in a school do not have their origins in the school, greater attention should be given to the development of linkages between school, home, community, and health and social welfare services. In addition, it recommended that providing a psychological service to schools would be a function of an intermediate educational tier.

Accordingly, the nucleus of this service will be established through the transfer and secondment to the education boards of members of the present Psychological Service and Guidance Inspectorate of the Department of Education.

In addition to contributing their specialist expertise to students and schools, the psychologists will also work as an integral part of the whole-school inspection team and will contribute, as required, to all other aspects of the Regional Inspectorate. They will be responsible for developing and promoting co-operation and linkages with other relevant local services, such as home-school links programmes and local health and welfare services.

A small group of psychologists will work in the Department of Education, as part of the restructured Central Inspectorate.

Secondment to the Inspectorate

Within the allocation of teachers in a region, some teachers with recognised competence and commitment will be seconded for specific periods on a contract basis to the Regional and Central Inspectorates.

Implementation of Changes

The proposals set out in this White Paper involve fundamental change for the inspectorate and for its relationship with schools. The future development of the Central and Regional Inspectorates will be supported by professional training programmes. These programmes will focus on intensive induction training, complemented by regular in-career training aimed at the development of their new roles and responsibilities and the provision of the specialist expertise necessary to carry out the proposed new functions for inspectors.

16 **The Department of Education**

Context

Many aspects of the administration of Irish education are very centralised. The roots of this centralisation lie deep. With the establishment of the commissioners for National Education in 1831 and of the Commissioners for Intermediate Education in 1878, a strong tradition emerged of powers and regulations residing in the Dublin offices of these authorities. The establishment of the Department of Education in 1924, with responsibility, under the Minister for Education as "corporation sole," for all educational sectors, led to a great accumulation of powers and functions within the Department.

The massive expansion of the education system since the 1960s has led to a huge increase in the day-to-day engagement of the Department with the rapidly expanding system. Although some organisational changes were made, such as the establishment of the Higher Education Authority, these changes did not keep pace with the extent of the transformation of the wider education system. Given the volume of executive work involved and the staff resources available, the Department has been unable to give the amount of attention necessary to policy analysis, policy development, strategic planning and evaluation of outcomes which should be its main concerns.

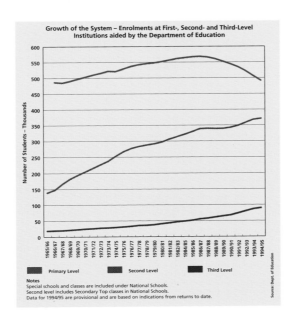

Growth of the System – Enrolments at First-, Second- and Third-Level Institutions aided by the Department of Education

Primary Level   Second Level   Third Level

Source: Dept. of Education

Notes
Special schools and classes are included under National Schools.
Second level includes Secondary Top classes in National Schools.
Data for 1994/95 are provisional and are based on indications from returns to date.

The excessive involvement of the Department in the day-to-day administration of the education system led the OECD in its ***Review of Irish Education*** in 1991 to the view that "*the Department of Education functions like a classic, highly centralised bureaucracy*" (p. 36). The OECD also observed that "*the case for devolution with respect to the functioning of the Department is . . . worth considering. Having shed what amount to largely managerial functions, it could then concentrate on higher-level administration and policy-oriented tasks. That is a measure that has been adopted in several OECD countries in recent years*" (p. 41).

This thinking is reflected in the proposals of this White Paper. While it is clear that the Minister for Education must remain ultimately responsible to the Oireachtas for the State's role in education, a major thrust of the White Paper is that the responsibility for the delivery of educational services should be devolved to regional or school and institutional level, where possible. The role of the Department should be changed to focus on strategic planning and policy and on the execution of those activities most efficiently conducted at national level. The Minister and Department, subject to the scrutiny of the Oireachtas, will also continue to act as the ultimate custodian of the public interest.

These new administrative proposals will have important implications for the Department itself as well as for the new regional tiers and for schools and other educational institutions. The ***Report on the National Education Convention*** noted that "*the restructuring of the Department of Education, the establishment of intermediate educational authorities and the promotion of Boards of Management with more autonomy would lead to a very changed administrative profile for the Irish education system. In the view of the Secretariat, the planned legislation would need to set out clearly the rights and responsibilities of each agency*" (p. 14). The subsequent ***Report on the Roundtable Discussions*** noted that "*if the planned new administrative structure for Irish education comes into existence, then a new set of relationships will be required between the three tiers – Centre, Region and Local*" (p. 25). The ***Report*** identified the need to make more explicit the precise nature of the linkages envisaged between the three tiers in the system.

The relationships between the education boards and schools and colleges are detailed elsewhere in this White Paper. The relationship between the Department of Education and regional and school or college levels will be determined by the functions and powers which remain appropriate to the national level. It is necessary therefore to address those functions and powers which are most appropriately conducted at national level and which will remain within the Department itself.

Strategic Management Initiative

The Department of Education has already commenced an examination of its existing internal structure and organisation as part of the Strategic Management Initiative launched by the Government in 1994. This examination and the policy review outlined in this White Paper have facilitated a formulation of the Department's mission as follows:

The mission of the Department of Education is to ensure the provision of a comprehensive, cost-effective and accessible education system of the highest quality, as measured by international standards, which will:

- **enable individuals to develop to their full potential as persons and to participate fully as citizens in society and**

- **contribute to social and economic development.**

One particular conclusion which emerged from the examination of activities carried out by the Department in the Strategic Management Initiative was the need to focus more sharply on outcomes and associated measures of performance and effectiveness. In a number of cases measures of performance are used in the Department which assess the efficiency of the delivery of a particular service, rather than the effectiveness of the service in satisfying higher-level objectives. This is a commentary on the limited resources applied to research in Ireland which could evaluate the effectiveness of specific programmes or education initiatives. It also reflects in part the absence of valid internationally accepted comparators which could enable a proper benchmarking exercise to be carried out. It also underlines, of course, that it is the wider education community (parents, teachers, students, institutions), and indeed society generally, not the Department, who are the primary determinants of educational outcomes.

Development of international comparators is receiving attention at present. Considerable progress has been made in recent years, through the work of the OECD on educational statistics and comparative indicators, in the comparison of different national systems of education at a macro level. It is possible to compare systems in terms of inputs (expenditure, staffing), results (graduation), outputs (student achievement, labour market outcomes) and processes (rates of participation, pupil-teacher ratios and indicators of school decision making). However, much work remains to be done in developing these indicators which have been published in *Education at a Glance* by the OECD in 1992, 1993 and 1995. Areas such as time spent in school, teacher remuneration, participation in continuing training and adult education will be covered in future OECD publications. Comparative work has also been undertaken by other international agencies such as UNESCO, the Council of Europe and Eurostat.

Another issue emerging from the Strategic Management Initiative is that many Departmental objectives as expressed have tended to be qualitative and generalised, not lending themselves readily to the development of performance indicators. However, it is important to have such indicators in order to establish, after a period of time, whether an objective had been met or the degree of progress being made towards its achievement. In the future, programmes which receive support from European Union Structural Funds will require explicit performance measures of their output. It has therefore been recognised that the Department needs to address as a priority the development of more appropriate performance indicators than those currently available, even though this task will in many instances be very difficult.

The development of **performance measures** – a critical part of strategic planning – is now being addressed in the context of the extension of the remit of the Comptroller and Auditor General to require a Value for Money system in all Government Departments. Within the Department of Education a Value for Money process has been initiated in order to put in place and implement the appropriate systems, procedures and practices necessary to evaluate the effectiveness of the Department's various activities and programmes. The Value for Money process will seek to establish core and other objectives for individual sections and for the Department as a whole in order to:

● identify the priorities of the divisions within the Department with regard to economy, efficiency and effectiveness of the divisions and their activities

● further the process of the establishment of meaningful performance measures and indicators and targets against which progress towards the attainment of objectives can be measured

● formulate mechanisms of periodic monitoring and critical scrutiny of performance

● develop further management information systems capable of delivering reliable data to underpin the system of performance review.

Role of the Department of Education

In the new planned administrative framework the Department will concentrate on its core functions and carry out those executive functions which are most efficiently conducted at national level. It will also be responsible for managing the relationships with a number of key external agencies, including other Government departments.

Core functions

The core functions of the Department will be:

● strategic planning and policy formulation for the system as a whole

● determination of national curricula

● promotion of equality throughout the system

● quality assurance

● resource allocation and appropriate monitoring

● evaluation of performance and outcomes

● determination of overall personnel policies for the system

● certain executive activities.

The ***Report on the National Education Convention*** noted the Department's intention to concentrate *"its work on strategic educational policy-formulation, on the maintenance of educational standards and accountability for* *them, on overall budgetary responsibility and support for those in greatest need of extra support and attention"* (p. 15). The **Report** went on to record that *"None of the presentations at the Convention questioned the wisdom of the main proposals for restructuring the Department . . ."* (p. 16).

Strategic Planning and Policy Formulation

The Department is responsible for providing the Minister with the best possible advice on education policy. The Department is required to formulate, develop and review alternative policy options for consideration by the Minister, and to devise plans for the effective implementation and evaluation of approved policy.

The increased capacity of the Department to perform these tasks will be strengthened by a number of measures. Internal reorganisation will enhance and develop the strategic policy units. In addition, as detailed elsewhere in the White Paper (See Chapter 15), a policy division will be established within the Central Inspectorate, and more structured links with educational research findings will be established.

In the context of continual social, economic and cultural development, the Department will advise the Minister on developing and making explicit the national educational policy framework within which all the partners in the education system will determine and develop their roles and responsibilities.

Resource Allocation and Monitoring

The main source of funding in the education system remains the central Exchequer. The Minister for Education is answerable to the Dáil with respect to Exchequer expenditure on education. Therefore, the Department of Education must retain overall budgetary responsibility for the system. In addition, the extension of the remit of the Comptroller and Auditor General into effectiveness auditing requires the development of processes for all areas of education which facilitate the evaluation of effectiveness and value for money while respecting the academic autonomy of the various institutions.

The Department will set out the **overall budgetary framework** within which each institution will determine the financial management of its affairs. The Department, through the education boards, the Higher Education Authority and the Further Education Authority as appropriate, will be responsible for ensuring that effective financial and accountability arrangements and internal control systems are in place within each institution, including the statutory identification of Accounting Officers at various levels of the system.

Evaluation of Performance and Outcomes

The Department is currently limited in its ability to evaluate the effectiveness of specific programmes or education initiatives. It is intended to increase the emphasis on the development of performance measurements throughout the education sector and this will be addressed through the Value for Money initiative. This work will be supported by improved linkages with educational research (see section below dealing with Research and Development).

All publicly funded institutions will be statutorily obliged to provide statistical data to the Department, as appropriate. This provision will also apply to institutions which receive a limited degree of State funding but are not funded predominantly from State sources and to other institutions availing of State certification.

Quality Assurance

The Central Inspectorate will be the main agency for overall quality assurance at first and second levels. The Audit Unit of the Central Inspectorate, as set out elsewhere in this White Paper, will evaluate and report on the standards and quality of the delivery of educational services. The Chief Inspector will report regularly on the functioning of the system and these reports will be published.

As outlined in Chapter 5, the Higher Education Authority will have overall responsibility for quality assurance in the third-level sector and will report on this to the Minister.

Promotion of Equality

The principle of equality is a cornerstone of national educational policy. Where participation and achievement in the education system are impeded by physical, health, intellectual, gender, economic or social factors, the system must act at every level to eliminate or compensate for the sources and consequences of educational disadvantage. The Department of Education will continually evaluate the operation of the education system to ensure that equality is being promoted. In addition, the Department will develop and support initiatives addressed specifically towards assisting those who would otherwise be prevented from participating in full in the education system.

Determination of National Curricula

The Department will be responsible for determining national curricula in all primary and second-level schools. The curricula will be based on advice from the National Council for Curriculum and Assessment, which will also have a range of advisory functions related to curriculum development and methods of assessment.

Certificate Examinations

The Department will continue to be responsible for administering the Certificate Examinations (including the Leaving and Junior Certificate Examinations) and for supervising other approved forms of assessment leading to national certification at second level.

Personnel Policy

Overall personnel policy for the entire education sector will remain a key responsibility of the Department. This will include responsibility for the negotiations of terms and conditions of employment for teachers as well as for the development of policies for in-career training and development of teachers.

Executive Functions

The Department at present carries out a number of executive functions, including:

- teachers' payroll

- administration of national examinations

- school transport

- planning and building service for primary and second-level schools, for regional and technological colleges and, in consultation with the Higher Education Authority, for the universities

- psychological service for primary and second-level schools.

The Department operates the payroll for most teachers; hence it is the biggest payroll operator in the State, paying out over £800 million per year.

The administration of teachers' payroll and the Certificate Examinations will remain within the Department. **Consideration will be given to including the teachers' payroll administered by the Vocational Education Committees in the national payroll**. Most of the remaining executive functions will be devolved outside the Department in the longer term.

The responsibility for the day-to-day administration and delivery of **school transport services** will remain with Bus Éireann, which will liaise with the education boards in relation to regional delivery requirements, in accordance with national policy and criteria laid down by the Department.

The establishment of priorities and budgets for **building** at all levels will remain within the Department as will the responsibility for major projects at primary and second level. Implementation of smaller projects and building maintenance at primary and second level will be devolved to the relevant education board or school, as appropriate.

School **psychological services** will be provided by the education boards.

Remit of the Ombudsman

Under the terms of the Ombudsman Act, 1980, the Department of Education comes under the remit of the Ombudsman. The remit of the Ombudsman will be **extended to the education boards** to facilitate accountability to those served by education boards, including parents, students and the wider community. **The extension of the Ombudsman's remit to all schools and colleges at first, second and third level, will also be explored**.

External Relationships

The Department will continue to work with other Government departments and outside agencies where appropriate. There are key linkages with a number of other Government departments including the Departments of Finance (funding), Enterprise and Employment (training), Justice (young offenders), Health (health promotion and child care) and Arts, Culture and the Gaeltacht (Irish Language, Arts). In the international context, the Department of Education will deal directly with the European Union on issues of European education policy and European funded programmes and with the OECD in the development of international education comparators. The Department will continue to develop and retain linkages with the education partners and social partners.

In diagrammatic form the future role of the Department will appear as follows:

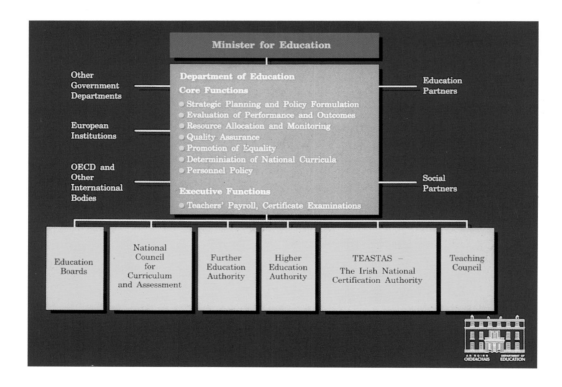

Implementation

Implementation of the new administrative framework will require a fundamental reorganisation of the Department, on the following lines:

- the development and strengthening of the capacity of the Department in the critical strategic areas of policy formulation, policy evaluation, budgetary and financial management, quality auditing and standards

- the development and putting in place of effective, linked and transparent systems of accountability at all levels of the system, with suitably qualified personnel and the development of policy performance measures, quality indicators and comprehensive management and financial information systems

- the development of structures and processes to ensure that the staff skills and competencies in the Department are adequate for the new challenges which it will face

- the development of improved communications systems, with the Department's external environment and internally

- the support of Departmental structures with the most appropriate and modern information technology systems.

The **Report on the National Education Convention** stressed that "*the restructuring of the Department of Education in line with new priorities, and its disengagement from its 'excessive involvement in day-to-day administration of the education system' will require time and care to ensure that the transition can be accomplished efficiently*" (p. 16). The restructuring of the Department will be carried, out on a phased basis, in line with the evolution of responsibilities at the other levels of the system. The Strategic Management Initiative will be used to define the details of the organisational framework for the new role of the Department.

Research and Development

Research and Educational Change

Research can be a potent agent of change. It provides a basis for questioning assumptions, problem identification, the evaluation of alternatives and the assessment of the outcomes. When linked with relevant research, the process of policy making facilitates and supports effective change. Research also provides for and underpins a creative continuity within the education system. By providing continual feedback of information to the system, educational research sustains the beneficial aspects of the system while at the same time stimulating creativity and development.

Research in the Context of Policy Formulation

A key element of the framework for development set out in this White Paper is a significantly changed role for the Department of Education. As set out above, a central focus of the Department's work will be on strategic policy formulation and the evaluation of policy effectiveness.

This enhanced policy focus will be supported by a more systematic approach to the use of research in support of decision making and in the review of the effectiveness of policies and their implementation. Research will also, in future, be used more systematically to contribute to debate among the partners on policy proposals.

The following principles will underpin the approach to educational research and development, in support of the department's overall policy role:

- clearer identification of research priorities to support major policy objectives and the allocation of resources to meet these priorities

- the development and promotion of close linkages between educational research agencies and the Department, with the objective of ensuring that priority policy issues are supported by relevant research

- the establishment of a comprehensive data base on relevant educational research

- the putting in place of arrangements for the wider dissemination of research findings to concerned interests.

The focus of research, in this section, is on research in support of Departmental policy formulation and review. The overall objective is to link this research more clearly to policy objectives and review of programmes. Separately, it is recognised that the autonomy of research as part of third-level education needs to be preserved.

Action

As well as funding a number of specific research and development projects, the Department of Education also directly funds a number of research and development institutes – the Shannon Curriculum Development Centre, the Education Research Centre and Institiúid Teangeolaíochta Éireann. The Department also funds the colleges of education and the education departments of the universities, through the Higher Education Authority; and the City of Dublin Curriculum Development Centre, through the City of Dublin Vocational Education Committee.

As part of the overall restructuring of the Department of Education, arising from this White Paper, **structures will be put in place to more systematically link research and the policy-making process**. Funding of the various research agencies and the approval of their annual and long-term plans will be on the basis of **agreed priorities and budgets linked to those priorities**. Specific research initiatives will also be undertaken on the basis of agreed objectives and budgets.

Part

6

International Dimension

17 Irish Education and the International Dimension

Context

The development of a partnership approach among the concerned interests is a recurring theme in this White Paper. This partnership is based on a recognition that effective co-operation among the partners promotes the welfare of students, benefits the wider society and enhances the contribution of education to the democratic process through enabling communities to actively influence the decisions which affect them.

This partnership ethos, as well as a sense of national confidence in the value and strength of the Irish education system, informs Ireland's contribution and full participation in international education activities within the European Union, in other international organisations in the wider world and, very importantly, in initiatives designed to foster increased mutual understanding between the traditions on the island of Ireland. In addition, the education system at all stages will seek to promote increased awareness of important issues within Ireland, in Europe and in the wider world. Accordingly, the partnership framework, which characterises national education development, will be a feature of Ireland's participation in the community of world nations. Ireland has a considerable amount to offer from its experience of educational policy and practice. Equally, Ireland can learn a great deal from the experience of others.

Background

The formulation of a national education policy in a Western democracy, as the twenty-first century approaches, must be firmly set in an international context. Ireland as a sovereign state in a world community of interdependent nations must have an education policy which prepares its young people for the challenges which will face people everywhere at this era in world history.

A consciousness of the global context in which education takes place has been much in evidence in the debate on educational reform in recent years. The ***Report on the National Education Convention*** noted the outward-looking character of contemporary Irish education due to a variety of factors, such as, the multiplicity of cultural ties which have their roots in early Christianity in Europe, political relationships and the history of Irish people seeking work in many countries around the world.

Recent geopolitical developments, including major changes in Eastern Europe, concern about an apparent resurgence of racism, violence and xenophobia in many countries, and the focus on conflict resolution in the island of Ireland, serve to underline the importance of education in areas such as human rights, tolerance, mutual understanding, cultural identity, peace and the promotion of co-operation in the world among people of different traditions and beliefs. The threat to the global environment has focused attention on the importance of environmental education.

Ireland has contributed very actively to the educational work of international bodies including the United Nations, the Organisation for Economic Co-operation and Development and the Council of Europe. In turn, Irish educational policy making and education practice have benefitted from of the work of these bodies.

Ireland's membership of the European Union gives particular importance to the European dimension of education. The prospect of increasing integration within the European Union ensures that this aspect will assume an even greater importance in the future.

European Union

As Ireland approaches the twenty-first century, a strong sense of European citizenship increasingly complements a robust Irish identity. Ireland's links with Europe have deep historical roots. This European tradition, in Irish affairs, is reinforced in modern times through Ireland's membership of the European Union and its full participation, in partnership with the other Member States in policy-making at European level. Ireland's development is now linked in an integral way with the development of Europe. This poses no threat to our national identity. Rather it offers significant opportunities for growth and development in the broader European context. In the education sector, Ireland's commitment to the European ideal is manifested in:

● its active participation in a wide range of European education programmes

● its development partnership with the European Union, through the structural funds, designed to promote economic and social development.

The framework for the development of education outlined in this White Paper, embraces confidently the European ideal.

The European Dimension in Education

As a member of the European Union, Ireland is closely involved in education and training policy development at European level. A variety of programmes has fostered linkages between educational institutions and personnel in Ireland and other Member States. Ireland has participated fully in these programmes.

A European perspective enhances students' education. It cultivates respect for cultural, social and ethnic differences; it promotes enhanced mutual understanding; and it fosters a shared sense of a common European heritage.

Ireland will continue to contribute fully to education initiatives within the European Union. The education system, at all appropriate levels, will participate fully in the implementation of the various European education programmes.

In the current Structural Fund Programme, there is a firm alignment between European Union supported initiatives and national policy priorities. Examples of this alignment are support for early childhood programmes, in-career development and senior-cycle re-structuring. Thus the partnership framework for future development within Ireland is complemented by a partnership of Ireland with the other member states of the European Union.

Treaty on European Union

The Government policy on closer European integration, includes support for and active participation in European Union programmes in the area of education, training, innovation, research and development in education. The general objective of the Maastricht Treaty provisions, in relation to education, is to facilitate Community policies which contribute to the development of quality education and training and to the nurturing of the cultures of the Member States.

Community action in education and training is, in accordance with the principles of subsidiarity enshrined in the Treaty, complementary to that of the Member States. Article 126 provides that such action will fully respect *"the responsibility of the Member States for the content of teaching and the organisation of education systems and their cultural and linguistic diversity"*.

Article 130(a) describes a policy of reducing disparities between the various regions of the European Union. The Structural Funds promote the development of underdeveloped regions and seek to promote the entry into the labour market of young people.

The Community Initiatives are concerned with the vocational development of young people, particularly those at risk in the labour market, promoting the integration of women in both vocational training and employment, and developing easier access into the labour market for the disabled and disadvantaged.

The Treaty provides for measures to support a range of actions and policies. These include:

- developing the European dimension in education, particularly through the teaching of the languages of the Member States

- encouraging mobility of students and teachers by encouraging, for instance, the academic recognition of diplomas and periods of study

- promoting co-operation between educational establishments

- developing exchanges of information and experience on issues common to the education systems of the Member States

- encouraging the development of youth exchanges and of teacher exchanges

- encouraging the development of distance education.

Community Action Programmes in Education and Vocational Training

SOCRATES

In line with the framework provided by the Treaty, the European Parliament and the Council of Ministers adopted the SOCRATES Action Programme in education early in 1995. The actions under this proposal will focus on the development of higher-quality education and training and the promotion of European co-operation in education. Its specific objectives are:

- to develop the European dimension in education

- to promote improvement in the knowledge of languages of the European Union

- to promote co-operation between institutions in the Member States at all levels of education

- to encourage the mobility of teachers and students, and contacts among students

- to encourage academic recognition of qualifications and periods of study

- to encourage open and distance education and exchange of information and experience

- to foster exchanges of information and experience.

Education can contribute significantly to the promotion of mutual understanding and tolerance on the island of Ireland and between the peoples of Europe. The SOCRATES programme offers significant opportunities for the promotion of understanding and co-operation between schools and colleges, North and South, as well as with counterparts in the rest of the European Union.

Irish schools will be actively encouraged to participate in actions in the SOCRATES programme, which can contribute to greater awareness of our common heritage and in particular human rights, both on this island and in the European Union.

LEONARDO DA VINCI

The Council decision of December, 1994, establishing an action programme for the implementation of a European Community Vocational Training Programme, effectively involves the streamlining of a range of existing programmes. The new programme highlights the need to improve the quality of, and capacity for innovation in, vocational training as part of a strategy targeted at growth, competitiveness and employment. Special emphasis is being accorded to vocational guidance, language learning and the promotion of equal opportunities. The implementation of the programme will be undertaken jointly by the Minister for Education and the Minister for Enterprise and Employment. The education sector has a key role in the implementation of the policy objectives of the Leonardo da Vinci programme. Schools and third-level institutions will play a major part in ensuring the success of this programme in Ireland. The programme will give an opportunity to schools and third-level institutions to play an active role in the promotion of high-quality vocational training and provide a vehicle for the transfer of best practice.

Implementation

The Department of Education and the Department of Enterprise and Employment will put in place the **necessary co-ordinating mechanisms** to ensure the success of the Socrates and Leonardo Da Vinci programmes.

Structural Funds and the Education Sector

For the six-year period 1994 to 1999, Ireland has agreed with the European Union a major developmental programme of education measures as part of the Community Support Framework. Total expenditure on such measures over this period will be £1.5 billion. These measures are designed to develop the capacity of Ireland's education system to contribute more effectively to social and economic well-being. The key contribution of education to economic and social prosperity is fully recognised by the European Union and the Union has invested very substantially in Irish education, recognising it as a crucial factor in promoting Ireland's development and achieving increased economic and social cohesion within the Union as a whole.

The European Commission's **White Paper on Growth, Competitiveness and Employment** recognised the critical role of education and training in ensuring the continued competitiveness of the European economy. In formulating its approach to the Community Support Framework 1994-1999, the Government recognised the critical role of education and training in achieving its objective to maximise the potential of young people. This is demonstrated by the fact that European Social Fund aid for human resource development represents 35 per cent of total European Union aid for the Community Support Framework. Within the Operational Programme for Human Resources Development, programmes in the education sector account for 58 per cent of the European Union aid.

In the present allocation of Structural Funds for the period up to 1999 the education sector objectives are focused on:

● enhancing the capacity of the education system to deliver high-quality education and training

● targeting provision to those who are most disadvantaged in society.

In pursuance of these objectives priority has been given to measures which:

● maximise the participation of young people in the learning process at all levels and particularly those at risk of early school leaving or of becoming disadvantaged on the labour market. A particular feature in this regard will be the provision, for the first time, of funding for early childhood compensatory programmes, and measures to prevent early school leaving within the education sector by students still within the compulsory school cycle

● restructuring of the senior cycle to make it more responsive to the wider range of ability levels arising from increased participation rates in education

● enhancing the contribution of third-level education to economic and social development

● increasing the emphasis on labour market relevance and skill needs of the economy in third-level programmes

● providing long-term unemployed persons with skills needed to enhance their prospects of gaining employment or progression to further education and training

● improvement of the quality of education and training. This involves, for instance, the provision of resources for the most comprehensive programme ever undertaken of in-career development for teachers at all levels of education, and for the development of comprehensive national certification for vocational education and training programmes through the establishment of a regulatory and supervisory authority

● a major investment in capital development at second and third level, including, in particular, a significant level of investment in new teacher centres.

The priority being accorded by the Government to the development of a high-quality education and training system will lay a solid foundation for the continuous development of the system and enhance its capacity to meet rapidly changing economic and social needs.

The Structural Fund Programmes underpin the value of education and training to the creation of social cohesion and economic prosperity. The range of measures supported is a clear recognition that the acquisition of competencies and skills among people is at least as important a source of social and economic transformation as more traditional forms of capital accumulation.

The programmes will be implemented thoroughly and evaluated systematically, in close partnership with the European Union.

Educational institutions should be active participants in the formulation and implementation of all relevant Community programmes. This objective is being given particular effect in the Structural Fund Community Initiatives. Operational guidelines for those give specific recognition to the critical role of the education sector in the delivery of the various measures being proposed in the programmes.

These initiatives offer the education sector an opportunity to develop, on a transnational basis, new methods, approaches and new types of qualifications which will serve to inform the mainstream education and training schemes in Ireland.

North-South Co-Operation in Education

The peace process provides an important opportunity to encourage co-operation and mutual understanding between the two parts of Ireland in the area of education. The document, *A New Framework for Agreement*, published by the British and Irish Governments in February 1995, makes specific reference to the potential for harmonising certain aspects of areas such as education.

Co-operative ventures in higher education, in training, in education for mutual understanding and in education for specialised needs are examples of areas where co-operation will be pursued this year. The mutual recognition of teacher qualifications in the North/South context will now be pursued fully, taking account of the relevant European Union legislation in the matter. There are also opportunities for co-operation in the context of the Socrates and Leonardo da Vinci programmes as well as the Community Initiatives.

Education has been discussed at meetings of the Anglo-Irish Inter-Governmental Conference. These meetings provide the basis for the continuous development of appropriate co-operation between the two education systems, taking full account of the developments following on the publication of the Framework Document.

It is planned to actively **promote the further expansion of the European Studies Project**, particularly through its extension to primary schools and, encouraging and assisting the participation of more schools from disadvantaged areas in both jurisdictions

The Department of Education is actively examining how the principles of mutual understanding and co-operation which inform the European Studies Project can contribute to the development of the School Education aspects of Socrates. **Co-operation in the third-level sector** is also being strongly encouraged at institutional level.

Teacher exchange schemes have an important role to play in the promotion of greater mutual understanding. **The North/South teacher exchange scheme** which has been in operation since 1990 will be examined, in consultation with the appropriate authorities, to determine the possibility for further expansion.

International Dimension

Ireland will continue to participate actively in the work of a variety of other international bodies, which have an educational remit. They include, for instance, the Council of Europe, the Organisation for Economic Co-Operation and Development and UNESCO.

An important component of the international dimension of education is making young people aware of the nature and causes of underdevelopment in the world and about what needs to be done to bring about change in relation to the imbalance in wealth between rich and poor countries. The horrific degradations being suffered by children, women and men in the third world – the victims of war and famine – underline the importance of creating an awareness of development issues at all levels of the education system.

An aim informing policy formulation, educational practice and curriculum development at the different levels will be to create an **awareness of global issues, including the environment and third-world issues**. The objective will be to stimulate a commitment, by individuals and society as a whole, to necessary actions to respond to specific crises and equally importantly to search for and promote long-term solutions to the underlying problems.

Estoppel and Legitimate Expectation

Legitimate expectation and promissory estoppel are associated principles which are relevant to the approach to legislation. **Estoppel** arises where a person makes a promise or a representation as to intention to another, on which that other person acts. The representor is bound by that representation or promise.

Whereas estoppel is a well established legal principle, the **principle of legitimate expectation** is still in its early developmental stage. This presents particular difficulties in assessing its likely impact on legislation. Put simply, the principle allows a person to claim that, in view of the existence of a regular practice by a public authority, s/he is entitled to expect that it will continue.

The impact of these principles in formulating implementation provisions, while significant, should not be exaggerated. First, it is unlikely that the Courts would find that either of these principles could fetter the Oireachtas in carrying out its duty to legislate in the public interest. It would be an untenable situation if the Oireachtas could be denied the opportunity to legislate on a matter, merely because that matter was subject to a long-standing practice. Furthermore, it is arguable that, where there are objective reasons which justify a change of practice, the principles of legitimate expectation and estoppel could not be relied upon to prevent that change. This would be true particularly where the change of practice arises from a policy decision of the Government, backed by an Act of the Oireachtas.

Proportionality

The principle of **proportionality**, to a large extent, incorporates the principles of **fairness and reasonableness**. A concise statement of the principle is to the effect that in order to establish whether a provision of law is consonant with the principle of proportionality, it is necessary to establish, in the first place, whether the means it employs to achieve its aim correspond to the importance of the aim and, in the second place, whether they are necessary for its achievement. In the case of school governance, the aim, being to make it more democratic, effective and inclusive, is a worthy and important one. Legislative provisions should strike a balance between the importance of that aim and the extent to which they will directly affect established interests.

Equality

Article 40.1 of the Constitution states:

All citizens shall, as human persons, be held equal before the law. This shall not be held to mean that the State shall not in its enactments have due regard to differences of capacity, physical and moral, and of social function.

This Article does not mean that everyone must be treated in the same way. However, in the context of school governance, in drafting legislative provisions which may have the effect of treating one school differently from another, care must be taken to ensure that any such differentiation is **proportionate** to its intended purpose and should also be proportionate to the difference between the schools. The criteria for distinguishing one school from another should be reasonable, known to all schools, and should lead to a situation where schools in similar circumstances are treated equally.

Denominational Education

The education system has developed along denominational lines. The majority of schools are denominational in their governance, structures and operation. Given this history of development and various provisions in the Constitution, there must be the strongest of presumptions that this structure and its support by State funding are constitutionally sound; that the Constitution supports the rights of parents to send their children to denominational schools and that the State provides funding for these schools in the context of its duty to provide for free primary education. Articles 40, 42 and 44 of the Constitution, and its Preamble, have implications for the State funding of a denominational system of education. The relevant sections of the Articles, and the Preamble, are quoted in an appendix to this chapter.

The provisions of these Articles appear to conflict in many respects. In particular, there could be a conflict between the provisions of Article 42, which acknowledges the primary role of parents in the education of their children, and the guarantees to religious denominations in Article 44, as regards the management of their own affairs, which would include their involvement in education. There is also an apparent tension between the prohibition in the Constitution on the endowment of religion and the implicit recognition in the Constitution of a denominational system of education. There may also be conflict between the provisions prohibiting discrimination on the grounds of religion and the rights of denominational schools to preserve a particular denominational ethos. The doctrine of harmonious interpretation may have a particular relevance in any consideration of issues relating to denominational education.

The relevant provisions of Article 40 are those relating to the holding of each citizen as equal before the law with due regard to differences of capacity and of social function. Article 42 acknowledges the special role of parents in the education of their children, including religious and moral education. This Article also provides constitutional support for a system of education which is privately owned but publicly funded and obliges the State to provide for free primary education. Article 44 is of particular importance given its provisions relating to freedom of religious practice, endowment of religion, discrimination on grounds of religion and the protection of the property of religious denominations.

The constitutional underpinning of denominational education has implications for school governance, student admission policies, staffing of schools and the funding of multi-denominational schools. It also has implications for what is referred to as the ethos of schools and how ethos is to be protected and fostered, while at the same time observing the constitutional right of children not to attend religious instruction.

Provisions in legislation relating to **school governance** should be such as will not unreasonably restrict schools in reflecting a particular denominational character. In practice, it is difficult to see how any reasonable proposals in this area would have this effect, given the commitment of patrons/ trustees/ owners/ governors, the majority of parents who send their children to denominational schools and the staff in those schools to preserving their ethos. In so far as proposals might be regarded as a dilution of the role of the denominational patrons/ trustees/ owners/ governors of schools in their governance and thus the denominational character of the schools, they must be a reasonable and proportionate response to the need to balance the rights of those patrons/ trustees/ owners/ governors against the rights of others with a significant interest in and commitment to the educational system, notably parents and teachers.

The denominational character of schools is a factor which plays a role in the admissions policies and staffing of schools. That role, however, must be reasonable and proportionate to the legitimate aim of preserving the ethos of schools and must balance this right of schools and their students against the rights to education of students of different denominations or none and the rights of teachers to earn a livelihood. While the denominational nature of schools may imply that they have a right to give preferential treatment to co-religionists, discrimination cannot be arbitrary and schools must act reasonably and fairly according to admissions and staffing criteria known to all in advance. The basis for such criteria could be set down, in broad terms, in legislation, while schools would provide the details as appropriate to their circumstances.

Multi-denominational schools have the same rights to funding as other schools, and any distinction in funding must not be based on their multi-denominational character.

School Governance - Legislation and Implementation

Given the range of interests involved in education, each of which has rights and duties, there is clearly the potential for competition and conflict. The aim of any proposals should be to avoid that competition by striking a balance which allows all parties to the educational system to participate in the governance of schools in proportion to their interest, thus channelling energies which might otherwise be dissipated through disagreement into constructive action for the good of the schools.

The first issue which must be addressed in the context of governance is the extent to which the State has the right, or even an obligation, to prescribe standards and structures for the governance of schools. The Oireachtas is, of course, entitled to legislate on any matter, subject only to the provisions of the

Constitution. The State, by virtue of its role as promoter and guardian of the common good, could reasonably be expected to ensure that the rights and interests of all the partners in the educational system are reflected in the basic element of that system, the individual school, in a way which gives due weight to each and to ensure that schools operate to the highest levels of effectiveness and efficiency. In addition, in view of the State's role in providing most of the funding for schools, there must be confidence on the part of the State agencies providing that funding that there are appropriate structures in place in schools to ensure that public funds are used in the manner intended. For these reasons, the authority of the State to enact legislation relating to school governance seems beyond doubt, subject to any provisions being proportionate and objectively necessary in the interests of the common good.

If the State, through the Oireachtas, has the authority to legislate for school governance, it must also have the authority to take all reasonable steps to ensure that the will of the Oireachtas is carried into effect. The precise implementation provisions will be worked out in the context of drafting legislation, but, given the nature of the education system, they are likely to focus on funding. Any legislative provisions which seek to ensure that schools have appropriate governance structures must conform to legal principles such as fairness, reasonableness and proportionality. In addition, the concepts of legitimate expectation and promissory estoppel would have a role to play. Finally, the provisions of the Constitution are relevant, particularly those relating to equality and the position of advancement of the common good in the constitutional scheme.

School Governance and Property Rights

It is not intended that provisions relating to school governance should in any way affect the title of owners of school property. The present legal arrangements, typically involving leases and trusts, would remain in place. The right of ownership of private property carries with it the right to decide how it is used. A requirement that schools have management boards, the composition of which is regulated by statute, need not amount to an improper or unconstitutional infringement of that right. To the extent that there would be any restriction on the right, it would be very much a *de minimis* one, affecting the activity in the schools, rather than any property right in them. As such, it should be reasonable and justifiable in the interests of the common good, objectively determined.

The Constitutional Rights of Parents

Article 42.1 states:

The State acknowledges that the primary and natural educator of the child is the family and guarantees to respect the inalienable right and duty of parents to provide, according to their means, for the religious and moral, intellectual, physical and social education of their children.

In their purest form, these provisions support the right of parents to educate their children privately, at home or in schools, with minimum involvement by the State. In practice, few parents have the resources to do this. In entrusting their children to schools, which for the most part are privately owned but publicly funded, **it should not be assumed that parents have in any way waived their constitutional rights**; indeed, the constitution itself refers to these rights as "inalienable". In bringing forward proposals for school governance, a central aim is to give a practical acknowledgement to the rights of parents, giving due weight to those rights in the educational system and allowing parents an opportunity to make that contribution to their children's education which is not only the wish of most parents but also their constitutional right and duty.

Affairs of Religious Denominations

Given the history of the educational system and the denominational character of much of it, it is likely that education could be regarded as part of the affairs of religious denominations, the management of which, by the denominations themselves, is guaranteed by Article 44.2.5 of the Constitution which states:

Every religious denomination shall have the right to manage its own affairs, own, acquire and administer property, movable and immovable, and maintain institutions for religious or charitable purposes.

However, education of their children is clearly also part of the affairs of parents whose primacy as educators is acknowledged in Article 42.1. Given the role of the State as guardian and promoter of the common good, education also forms an important part of the affairs of the State, as demonstrated by the large amounts of public funds devoted to it. These competing interests must be resolved in a way which is both constitutionally satisfactory and practicable. The resolution certainly should not lie in allowing the rights of any one group a supremacy over the right of others. Instead it should lie in a set of proposals which seek to interpret and apply the constitutional provisions in harmony with each other, achieving in the process a balance between the rights and duties of all.

The Role of the State in the Delivery of Education

The importance of education to the social and economic wellbeing of society is evidenced by the general agreement which exists with regard to the devotion of substantial resources from the Exchequer to education. Given its role in allocating these resources, the State must be in a position to play a significant role, on behalf of children and their parents and in the interests of the common good generally, in setting and enforcing standards. In addition, the State is obliged by the Constitution to require that children receive a certain minimum education. This inevitably must involve setting out criteria relating to the content of the curriculum and the teaching methods and standards in schools funded by the State. In carrying out its constitutional duty, however, the State must have regard to the constitutional rights of parents, especially where they choose to educate their children otherwise than in schools funded by the State.

Outline of Legislative Provisions

General Format

The general approach to legislation will be a combination of detailed provision, where this is desirable but within a general scheme of provisions, which will be a more flexible statement of principles with provision for back-up in the form of regulations, rules and directives. Legislation will be introduced for:

Governance

The legislation will provide that schools, in receipt of public funds shall have a board of management, the powers and functions of which shall be prescribed. The legislation will also address the implementation of governance provisions, including provisions with the aim of ensuring a governance structures in line with the decisions in this White Paper.

Organisational Structure

A clear area for legislation is the organisational structure of the education system. Legislative provision will be made for education boards with responsibility for the administration of education at regional level (see chapter 14) and there will be reform of the Vocational Education Committee legislation. Provisions will detail the various bodies involved in education, for instance, parents, boards of management, education boards, Vocational Education Committees, and the Department of Education. It will also set out the roles and functions of the various bodies at the various levels in the education system, pre-school, first, second and third levels and further education. The role of the school in respect of school plans, the obligations of schools and education boards towards travellers, the responsibilities of the boards of management in respect of observance of the school year will be put on a statutory basis.

National Bodies

Legislation will provide for the new national educational bodies such as for TEASTAS – the Irish National Certification Authority, the Further Education Authority and the restructured Higher Education Authority. It will set out the composition, powers and functions of these and their links with each other and with other structures.

University Legislation

Legislation will also provide for new Governing Body-structure for universities, the restructuring of the National University of Ireland, and the putting in place of arrangements for appropriate public accountability.

Rules

A statutory basis will be given to the Rules for National Schools and other comparable rules and regulations and to the continuing authority of the Minister for Education, or in appropriate cases the education boards, to make regulations and issue directives with a view to implementing policy in the education system.

Teachers

Provisions relating to a Teaching Council and the teaching profession generally will be provided. These could include provisions relating to the position of teachers in schools and their duties and rights, particularly their rights in respect of discrimination and their right to earn a livelihood. The Council will have wide-ranging powers in relation to teacher discipline and recognition.

Appendices

Appendix 1 – Relevant Constitutional Provisions

Preamble

In the name of the Most Holy Trinity, from Whom is all authority and to Whom, as our final end, all actions both of men and States must be referred,

We, the people of Éire,

Humbly acknowledging all our obligations to our Divine Lord, Jesus Christ, Who sustained our fathers through centuries of trial,

Gratefully remembering their heroic and unremitting struggle to regain the rightful independence of our Nation,

And seeking to promote the common good, with due observance of Prudence, Justice and Charity, so that the dignity and freedom of the individual may be assured, true social order attained, the unity of our country restored, and concord established with other nations,

Do hereby adopt, enact, and give to ourselves this Constitution.

Article 40.1

1. All citizens shall, as human persons, be held equal before the law.

This shall not be held to mean that the State shall not in its enactments have due regard to differences of capacity, physical and moral, and of social function.

Article 42

1. The State acknowledges that the primary and natural educator of the child is the Family and guarantees to respect the inalienable right and duty of parents to provide, according to their means, for the religious and moral, intellectual, physical and social education of their children.

2. Parents shall be free to provide this education in their homes or in private schools or in schools recognised or established by the State.

3. 1 The State shall not oblige parents in violation of their conscience and lawful preference to send their children to schools established by the State, or to any particular type of school designated by the State.

2 The State shall, however, as guardian of the common good, require in view of actual conditions that the children receive a certain minimum education, moral, intellectual and social.

4. The State shall provide for free primary education and shall endeavour to supplement and give reasonable aid to private and corporate educational initiative, and, when the public good requires it, provide other educational facilities or institutions with due regard, however, for the rights of parents, especially in the matter of religious and moral formation.

5. In exceptional cases, where the parents for physical or moral reasons fail in their duty towards their children, the State as guardian of the common good, by appropriate means shall endeavour to supply the place of the parents, but always with due regard for the natural and imprescriptible rights of the child.

Article 44

1. The State acknowledges that the homage of public worship is due to Almighty God. It shall hold His Name in reverence, and shall respect and honour religion.

2. 1 Freedom of conscience and the free profession and practice of religion are, subject to public order and morality, guaranteed to every citizen.

2 The State guarantees not to endow any religion.

3 The State shall not impose any disabilities or make any discrimination on the ground of religious profession, belief or status.

4 Legislation providing State aid for schools shall not discriminate between schools under the management of different religious denominations, nor be such as to affect prejudicially the right of any child to attend a school receiving public money without attending religious instruction at that school.

5 Every religious denomination shall have the right to manage its own affairs, own, acquire and administer property, movable and immovable, and maintain institutions for religious or charitable purposes.

6 The property of any religious denomination or any educational institution shall not be diverted save for necessary works of public utility and on payment of compensation.

Appendix 2 – Relevant Extracts from the Government of Renewal Policy Document

48. White Paper on Training

We propose to publish at an early date a comprehensive White Paper on Training.

The White Paper will address the following:

- Investment in the continuing training of Irish workers' needs, to be brought up to levels equivalent to the best practices of our international competitors. We will involve the Social Partners in a dialogue as to how best this can be achieved;

- A unified national system for the certification of vocational training which will underpin training quality and improve trainee employability will be created;

- Progress will be made towards a national goal of making an offer of quality vocational training to young new entrants to the labour market, as a positive alternative to unemployment in the context of the EU Youth Start Initiative.

The Minister for Enterprise and Employment will initiate a major public debate on the White Paper's proposals, which will lead to the setting up of a National Training Certification Board.

When this process is completed, and the NTCB is established, it will become one of the constituent bodies of the National Education and Training Certification Board, legislation for which will be introduced by the Minister for Education during the lifetime of the Government.

100. EDUCATION

We are committed to a high quality education system which is democratically managed and publicly accountable, to which each person has equal access, and which enables people to return to education at various stages of their lives.

Among our priorities are:

- the completion and early publication of the White Paper on Education and the introduction of subsequent legislation;

- An examination of the use of educational buildings with particular reference to their retention in educational use;

- Further expansion of pre-school facilities, with the ultimate aim of an integrated professional national system linked to the primary school system;

- Significant reductions in class sizes in primary schools, with a special emphasis on areas of disadvantage;

- Increasing access to remedial, psychological, and Home School links services;

- Expansion of remedial and career guidance service at second level;

- Increased capitation grants for primary schools with a special emphasis on schools which include pupils from disadvantaged backgrounds;

- Schools to be facilitated in the ongoing testing of all pupils for diagnostic and remedial purposes;

- A commitment to the provision of ongoing in-service education for teachers;

- Support for multi-denominational schools and Gael-scoileanna including the early recognition of new schools;

- Introduction of new second-level curricula at present being devised by the NCCA, including adequate provision of teacher in-service training;

- Working towards the development of an element of school-based assessment in Junior and Leaving Certificate examinations;

- Encouragement of fee-paying schools to enter the free education system;

- Granting special consideration to the needs of schools enrolling children with handicaps or severe learning difficulties;

- Working towards the integration of targeted educational services, e.g., Youthreach, VTOS, Second-level, PLCs;

- Pilot initiatives to address the problems of truancy and early drop-out;

- Adequate provision for the establishment and maintenance of school-book loan schemes at primary and secondary level for disadvantaged pupils;

- The investment of special resources in adult literacy and adult education schemes;

- An examination of the needs and abilities of all children from disadvantaged backgrounds to encourage and facilitate their continued participation in education;

- New support mechanisms to increase participation by 3rd level students from low-income backgrounds, including the abolition of third-level fees, a comprehensive reform of the Higher Educational Grants Scheme, the introduction of support for students on Post-Leaving-Certificate courses, and an increase in the number of third-level places;

- A commitment to proceed with the proposed new Regional Technical Colleges. In the lifetime of this Government we will develop an urban college on the existing campus in Dún Laoghaire. We will establish the Tipperary Rural Business Development Institute. We will consolidate and develop the educational programme in Castlebar;

- The establishment of a comprehensive welfare service for teachers;

- The conclusion of negotiations on optional retirement for teachers and the expansion of job-sharing schemes;

- Legislation to regulate private education to ensure proper educational standards, consumer protection and employee rights;

- The development of the Stay Safe programme on a national basis;

- The establishment of a programme on Sexuality and Relationships by all schools at first and second level;

- Implementation of the Civic, Social and Political Studies Programme in all post-primary schools from September 1996;

- The promotion of gender equity with particular reference to curriculum and career choice;

- Increased funding for the National Parents' Councils (Primary and post-Primary) for administration and parent training for participation in Boards of Management.

120. An Ghaeilge

Is cuid lárnach de shaol agus de chultúr na hÉireann í an Ghaeilge, a bhí mar theanga dhúchais ag formhór ár muintire anuas go dtí an céad seo caite.

The Irish language has an integral and creative role to play in defining Irish identity. We accept that the State must play a leading role in expanding the degree of bilingualism in Irish society and, in particular, in achieving greater usage of Irish.

Má táthar chun úsaid na Gaeilge a leathnú, ní mór go mbrathfadh an pobal go gcuirfí fáilte roimh aon saoránach a bheadh ag iarraidh gnó a dheanamh leis an Státchóras trí mheán na Gaeilge.

We will continue to improve the availability of State services through Irish and bilingually, generally and especially for the people of the Gaeltacht. A list of services which will be provided through Irish or bilingually by the State will be drawn up by all Departments annually.

Bord na Gaeilge will continue with its programmes of action for these purposes, to be implemented by Government Departments and public sector agencies.

We will set up a Commission to review the work and effectiveness of Irish Language Organisations.

The staffing of An Gúm will be reviewed by the Management Services Unit of the Department of Finance, and their Report will form the basis on which An Gúm will transfer to the Department of Arts, Culture and the Gaeltacht.

Principal
References

Principal References

A Government of Renewal – A Policy Agreement between Fine Gael, the Labour Party and Democratic Left. Dublin, 1994.

A New Framework for Agreement. Government of Ireland, Dublin: The Stationery Office, 1995.

A Strategy for Competitiveness, Growth and Employment. National Economic and Social Council, Report No. 96, Dublin: National Economic and Social Council, 1993.

A Time for Change: Industrial Policies for the 1990s – Report of the Industrial Policy Review Group (the Culliton Report). Industrial Policy Review Group, Dublin: The Stationery Office, 1992.

Circular 20/90 – Guidelines towards a Positive Policy for School Behaviour and Discipline and *A Suggested Code of Behaviour and Discipline for National Schools.* Department of Education, Dublin: Department of Education, 1990.

Circular M33/91 – Guidelines towards a Positive Policy for School Behaviour and Discipline and *A Suggested Code of Behaviour and Discipline for Post-Primary Schools.* Department of Education, Dublin: Department of Education, 1991.

Curaclam na Bunscoile – Teacher's Handbook, Parts 1 and 2. Department of Education, Dublin: Browne and Nolan, 1971.

Education and Economy in a Changing Society. Organisation for Economic Co-operation and Development, Paris: OECD, 1989.

Education and Training Policies for Economic and Social Development. National Economic and Social Council, Report No. 95, Dublin: National Economic and Social Council, 1993.

Education at a Glance, OECD Indicators. Organisation for Economic Co-operation and Development – Centre for Educational Research and Innovation, Paris: OECD, 1992, 1993 & 1995.

Education for a Changing World. Government of Ireland, Dublin: The Stationery Office, 1992.

Employment through Enterprise – The Response of the Government to the Moriarty Task Force on the Implementation of the Culliton Report. Government of Ireland, Dublin: The Stationery Office, 1993.

Evaluation of the Community Support Framework from 1989-1993. Economic and Social Research Institute, Dublin: Economic and Social Research Institute, 1994.

Interim Report of the Technical Working Group of the Steering Committee on the Future Development of Higher Education. Steering Committee on the Future Development of Higher Education, Dublin: Higher Education Authority, 1995.

Ireland – Community Support Framework 1994 – 1999. European Commission, Brussels & Luxembourg: Office for Official Publications of the European Communities, 1994.

Ireland – National Development Plan 1994 •1999. Government of Ireland, Dublin: The Stationery Office, 1993.

Making Knowledge Work for Us – Report of the Science Technology and Innovation Advisory Council. Science Technology and Innovation Advisory Council, Dublin: The Stationery Office, 1995.

National Youth Policy Committee – Final Report. National Youth Policy Committee, Dublin: The Stationery Office, 1984.

OECD Jobs Study – Facts, Analysis, Strategies. Organisation for Economic Co-operation and Development, Paris: OECD, 1994.

Operational Guidelines for Structural Fund Community Initiatives. European Commission, Brussels & Luxembourg: Office for Official Publications of the European Communities, 1995.

Operational Programme (1994 – 1999) for Human Resources Development. Government of Ireland, Dublin: The Stationery Office, 1995.

Position Paper on Regional Education Councils. Dublin: The Department of Education, 1994.

Position Paper on the Governance of Schools. Dublin: The Department of Education, 1994.

Programme for Competitiveness and Work. Government of Ireland, Dublin: The Stationery Office, 1994.

Report on the National Education Convention. The Convention Secretariat, Dublin: The National Education Convention Secretariat, 1994.

Report of the Primary Education Review Body. Primary Education Review Body, Dublin: The Stationery Office, 1990.

Report of the Review Body of the Primary Curriculum. Review Body of the Primary Curriculum, Dublin: The Department of Education, 1990.

Report on the Roundtable Discussions on the Minister for Education's Position Paper on Regional Education Councils. John Coolahan and Seamus McGuinness, Dublin, 1994.

Report of the Special Education Review Committee. Special Education Review Committee, Dublin: The Stationery Office, 1993.

Review of National Policies for Education – Ireland. Organisation for Economic Co-operation and Development, Paris: OECD, 1991.

Rules for National Schools. Department of Education, Dublin: The Stationery Office, 1965.

School Attendance/ Truancy Report. Department of Education Working Group, Dublin: Department of Education, 1994.

Sport for All Charter. Council of Europe, Strasbourg: Council of Europe, 1978.

Survey of Research in the Higher Education Sector. Forfás, the Policy and Advisory Board for Industrial Development in Ireland, Dublin: Forfás, 1994.

Treaty on European Union (Maastricht Treaty). European Commission, Luxembourg: Office for Official Publications of the European Communities, 1992.

White Paper on Growth, Competitiveness and Employment. European Commission, Brussels & Luxembourg: Office for Official Publications of the European Communities, 1993.

United Nations Convention on the Rights of the Child. United Nations, Geneva: United Nations, 1990.

Constitution and Legislation

University of Dublin Charter, 1591

National University of Ireland Act, 1908

Ministers and Secretaries Act, 1924

School Attendance Acts, 1926 to 1967

Vocational Education Acts, 1930 to 1944

Bunreacht na hÉireann, Constitution of Ireland. Dublin: Government Stationery Office, 1937.

National Council for Educational Awards Act, 1979

Ombudsman Act, 1980

University of Limerick Act, 1989

Dublin City University Act, 1989

The Child Care Act, 1991

Dublin Institute of Technology Acts, 1992 and 1994

Regional Technical Colleges' Acts, 1992 and 1994

Notes